D1108748

"Every so often a reviewer is allotted a book he would like to have written himself. Such a book is *Death and Consciousness*. . . . The book deserves a wide readership."

David Christie-Murray
Light

"[An] excellent book about an intriguing subject . . . Highly recommended."
SSC Booknews

"A good introduction to someone new to the subject . . . If you like to explore this topic, and are interested in how survival relates to consciousness . . . this book is for you."

Jean Burns, PhD
PSI Research

DEATH AND CONSCIOUSNESS

DAVID H. LUND

*From the Library
of the*
John Fox Family

BALLANTINE BOOKS • NEW YORK

Library of Congress Catalog Card Number: 84-43211

ISBN 0-345-35178-9

This edition published by special arrangement with MacFarland & Co., Inc., Publishers, Jefferson, N.C.

Manufactured in the United States of America

First Ballantine Books Edition: April 1989

To my mother and father

CONTENTS

PREFACE

IN THE BOOK OF ECCLESIASTES WE READ, "THE LIVING know that they shall die." We are not in a position to question this somber feature of human experience. But what of Job's question, "If a man die shall he live again?" This question has been posed in some fashion or another by most people throughout the ages. It is an expression of the ultimate mystery and is of no less concern to us than it was to Job. We find ourselves wondering about whether our limited span of existence in this life is all the experience we shall ever have. Almost everyone at some time or another thinks deeply about this question. A correct answer would tell us not only whether or not we should expect a continuation of our existence after death but also much about the ultimate nature of reality and of our nature as human beings.

This most important question has seldom been posed clearly and unambiguously, or discussed objectively. Those who believe in survival of death because it is a dogma of their religion usually do so uncritically and are generally more concerned with persuading others to accept their belief than with trying to find out whether survival is a fact. On the other hand, those who reject this belief on the grounds that man is a completely material being, or that consciousness and personality are utterly dependent upon a living human body, may be just as uncritical in their thinking. Though one of these beliefs must be essentially correct and the other incorrect (i.e., either at least some people will survive death in some fashion or else they will not), anyone approaching this matter with an open mind must seek the reasons or evidential considerations which can be advanced for or against these beliefs.

Reports of strange occurrences suggesting that people have survived death have appeared throughout recorded history and have, within the last 100 years or so, been subjected to critical scrutiny by a number of careful and highly capable investigators. Many of these reports seem to indicate that some people who died have survived in some manner and have managed to communicate with the living. But a great number of people, including many who are intelligent and well-educated, dismiss this so-called evidence, mainly on the grounds that survival of death is impossible, and so there cannot be any genuine evidence for it. Consequently, these reports are not taken seriously. What I hope to do in the sequel is to present a view, based upon an examination of our nature as persons, about how people could conceivably survive death—about the experiences they could have and the world they could encounter—and thereby provide, among other things, reason for believing that at least some of these strange occurrences really do indicate what they seem to indicate about survival of death. I will try to show that those who claim that there cannot be life after death are mistaken—that life after death may very well be a reality and, at any rate, is not ruled out by any scientific findings or compelling arguments of a logical or philosophical nature.

In the first part of the book, I present (and, of course,

defend) a view of the nature of a person and the world he encounters which is not only compatible with the claim that a person survives death but suggests that survival is more than a remote possibility. Then, after having established the possibility of survival of death, I proceed, in the second part of the book, to consider various kinds of empirical evidence for thinking that this is actually the case; that is, that at least some deceased persons have *in fact* survived death and have managed to communicate that fact to the living.

I argue that mind cannot be reduced to matter, that persons are essentially of the nature of mind, that it is far from obvious that consciousness is generated by the brain, that a very significant portion of our experience of this world is mind-contributed, and that one can conceive of a plausible "next world" in which the self continues to generate experience but now in response to a non-material source of stimulation. What emerges is a view, based upon a careful examination of what we find ourselves to be in our experience of this world, in terms of which reports of survival in another world are readily understood.

1

Scope and Method
of the Study

A STUDY OF THE QUESTION OF HUMAN SURVIVAL OF death may seem extremely ambitious. After all, haven't great numbers of people from time immemorial been struggling to answer this question with limited or no success? If the question were one involving the psychology, sociology, or physiology of dying, it wouldn't be so difficult to answer. There is an increasing amount of literature dealing with the psychological and sociological aspects of dying, and this is, admittedly, an important area of study. The study of social attitudes, funeral customs, and methods of relating to the dying and the bereaved can be of considerable value. But the focus of this study lies elsewhere. Death presents itself as an enigma, the ultimate mystery. Does it destroy us? Or do we (whatever *we* are) survive it in some manner? The difficulty in trying to answer such questions is intensified by the fact that the study of death is not just one more academic area of study. Since death threatens us with personal annihilation, a considerable amount of psychological as well as intellectual honesty is required to see clearly in this area.

1

Perhaps the first point to note with respect to whether this question about survival is answerable is that we must not set our sights too high. We ought not count on arriving at an incontrovertible proof which yields complete certainty. Philosophers and others who have studied the basis and justification of our knowledge claims realize that such certainty is not justified even with respect to those matters which we would never seriously doubt. And so it should not be disappointing to have to look for something less than that—evidence, probabilities, good reasons for believing—which may justify belief without conferring a guarantee.

The importance of an open-minded attitude in a study of this kind cannot be overestimated. Most of the alleged occurrences relevant to survival are so bizarre, so shocking to the common sense of our time that it may be difficult to take them seriously. For they challenge our fundamental beliefs about the world. But we must be careful not to simply dismiss, without inquiry or reflection, that which is incompatible with our assumptions about the nature of the world. For these assumptions, regardless of how basic they are or how much we cherish them, may be mistaken, and in that case our refusal to consider any claim incompatible with them will act like blinders, keeping us from discovering the truth. One can maintain an open-minded attitude without becoming overly credulous and accepting claims without sufficient consideration of the evidence for them. The ideal is to maintain a readiness to consider claims that challenge one's assumptions, but in a critical, reflective way which leads one to draw conclusions in an intellectually responsible manner. In an emotionally-laden area there is a strong temptation to jump to conclusions rather than to draw them responsibly. If one hopes to survive death, it will be tempting for him to leap to that conclusion. On the other hand, there are those who wish to disbelieve in survival of death, and they may very well be tempted to jump to the opposite conclusion. But such temptations must be resisted. The issues involved are ultimately so important that wishful thinking in either direction must be kept to a minimum. Little is to be gained by deceiving oneself.

The question of the survival of death is a very large one. There are other questions and issues which must be addressed before this one can even be understood, much less answered. For example, one cannot proceed very far in an attempt to determine whether a person will survive death, or even to understand what it *means* to say that a person will survive his own death, without considering very carefully how we are to think of ourselves as persons. The issue as to the nature of a person is one that has certainly not been settled to the satisfaction of everyone. In some views of what it is to be a person, survival of death seems to be impossible. In most views there are serious difficulties which must be addressed. But, at any rate, if one hopes to answer the question in an intellectually responsible manner, then this issue, along with others, must first be formulated with greater precision and then the implications drawn with more logical rigor than is usually done in discussions of life after death.

Reflection on how we are to think of ourselves as persons will likely reveal to us implicitly held assumptions which cannot bear the light of critical scrutiny. There can be little doubt that the role of the physical body has been overemphasized in the thinking of a great many modern men and women, making it difficult for them to believe in or even think clearly about survival of death. Such excessive attention and emphasis is understandable in our scientific age. Since the very method of science leads it to attend to only the physical aspects of nature, as they are the only ones which can be publicly observed, the scientific study of man will be confined to an investigation of his bodily existence and characteristics. The scientific method requires the scientist to take the position of an outside or external observer. When a scientist looks at another human being, he does not observe with his senses that person's consciousness or self-awareness. Only the person's physical characteristics and bodily behavior are publicly observable and thus accessible to the scientific method. Even the psychologist, if he ignores the testimony of introspection, will confine himself to this external approach. Such an exclusive preoccupation with the "outside" or publicly observable aspects of the individual leads to doubts about the very existence of the "inner" self or "I"—that which the person finds himself to be in the process of having any experience. The concept of the physical or "scientific" object, the public object viewed from without, creeps surreptitiously into our conceptual framework and shapes our concept of what it is for something to be real. We come to think of reality in physical terms, and everything else tends to slip between the meshes of our conceptual net. Thus it is not surprising that, rather uncritically, we come to think of ourselves only as bodies.

Of course, such a conclusion does not follow. We ought not expect to come upon the self in that manner. We cannot photograph it or take physical measurements of it. As we shall see, to think clearly about our own nature, we must abandon the perspective of the external observer and concentrate upon our experience of self-consciousness. We must introspect or turn within to our own states of consciousness in our effort to discover the existence and nature of the self. At this point we must leave behind the scientific method, insofar as this method is applicable only to publicly observable phenomena. For self-consciousness is directly observable only by the one whose self-consciousness it is. No one else can directly apprehend our conscious states. They are only privately observable.

Self-consciousness is a reality whose existence we are not in a position to deny. It is a most fundamental feature of our world. As such, it should be of great concern to science. But its privacy renders it unamenable to the scientific method. Equally undeniable, although also private, is the reality of self-identity—our awareness of remaining one and the same being throughout our various experiences. These realities are so fundamental to experience, so close to our being, that, almost incredibly, we often miss them as we look outward to the world of physical objects, without realizing that they are the conditions which make such observation possible. If the scientific observer should doubt this, we might remind him that he is a person and that if he introspects he will not be able to doubt the reality of his own self-conscious being. It seems that there are those who are prone to forget that the scientific enterprise is carried on by self-conscious beings, and not by some impersonal investigative process.

Though our method of investigation cannot be confined to the methods of scientific investigation, we must pay close attention to what science has discovered about our brains and bodies, and to what it knows about the natural laws which govern our world. But we must also be very attentive to what it doesn't know, and perhaps cannot know, in the areas of concern to us, lest we be misled by failing to carefully distinguish between what it has definitely established and what we, perhaps automatically and unjustifiably, assume or take for granted.

A philosophical approach involving an analysis of the crucial concepts and a critical examination of some of our fundamental assumptions about the nature of reality are essential. We cannot overestimate the importance of carefully examining the central concepts in terms of which we think about survival. Though such an undertaking alone may not provide any evidence for or against survival, it will help us to think clearly about what it would be to survive death and to dispel doubts about whether we have anything intelligible in mind when we talk about it. And the disclosure and critical examination of what we are assuming, perhaps unconsciously, about the nature of reality will help to eliminate confusion about and objections to survival based upon unfounded assumptions. Since our survival depends upon our nature as persons and the natural law of our world, any assumptions or beliefs about these matters should be based upon the most judicious examination that we are in a position to undertake.

2

THE CASE AGAINST BELIEF IN SURVIVAL

As we begin to wonder about our chances of experiencing some sort of life after death, they may seem to be very poor indeed. Apart from religious faith in a God who will prevent our permanent destruction by death, there may seem to be no basis for believing in a life after death. When death occurs there is an irreparable breakdown of the biological functions. The heart stops, the brain dies, and all the vital processes cease. All observable evidence of human life in the body disappears. Our observation of a corpse certainly suggests that the person who once animated it is not in existence any longer.

But, perhaps, it will be said, the *soul* or *spirit* lives on. Perhaps the person is still in existence and still conscious, but simply unable to communicate with us now that the body is dead. Since we communicate via our bodies and sense organs, it should not be surprising that communication ceases with the death of the body.

However, there are a number of empirical facts which appear to rule out this possibility, as they suggest that consciousness depends for its existence upon a living organism. Some of these facts are commonly observed and others are revealed to us by the natural sciences. The fact that all signs of consciousness cease to occur when the body dies is one that anyone can observe. Moreover, it is obvious that even while the body is living, a blow to the head may temporarily have the same result. Science has gone further in showing that damage to specific areas of the brain results in the elimination or impairment of particular mental capacities and that the capacities for seeing, hearing, tasting, smelling and touching are connected, in the case of each, with a different region of the brain. Drugs such as LSD, mescaline, psilocybin, and heroin alter consciousness in a profound way by altering brain and body chemistry. And when portions of the brain are radically disconnected with the rest, as in the case of a prefrontal lobotomy, significant changes in consciousness and personality result. Thus the dependence of consciousness on brain and body seems difficult to deny.

The advance of science has made it more difficult to believe in a life after death. It has given support to the argument that we do not know of anything in us or about us which could survive. One might argue that science does not know of any non-physical entity "in" us which is immune to death. It doesn't know of any soul or spirit or consciousness that continues to exist after death of the body. The heart dies, the entire body dies and decomposes. So what is left over? What is there in us which could survive? The answer seems to be "Nothing whatsoever."

In addition to these considerations, there are some widely accepted theories about the relationship between consciousness and the body which, if true, would effectively rule out survival of death. One theory, which we may call the electrochemical theory of consciousness, holds that consciousness is nothing other than the electrical and chemical events taking place in the neural tissue of the brain. In this theory all of our feelings, thoughts, volitions, and sensations are identical with brain processes. The obvious implication of this theory is that when the brain and body die, consciousness must also cease to exist.

Another theory equates mind and consciousness with behavior. In this view, an animal's consciousness of the difference between two objects is identical with the difference in its behavior toward each. A dog's consciousness of the difference between, say, an electric fence and its food dish *consists in* the difference in its behavior when in the presence of these objects. Though this view has some plausibility when applied to lower animals, it may seem to lose whatever plausibility it has when applied to us; for we frequently engage in mental activity which has no obvious behavioral correlate. When we are lost in thought our bodies may be quite motionless, not engaging in any obvious behavior. However, a defender of this view would claim that even though we are not displaying any overt behavior, as we would be if we were speaking, there is nevertheless a micro-behavior taking place which consists in minute motions in the larynx and vocal cords. So in this view all thoughts, all mental activity is nothing but behavior and thus must cease when the body dies.

Another argument against life after death centers around the claim that we cannot imagine or even conceive of what possible form that existence could take. This seems to be a very powerful objection. Without a body we couldn't have any physical sense organs. But it seems obvious that the sense organs are necessary for sense experience. Can we conceive of ourselves seeing without eyes, hearing without ears, etc.? It appears that we cannot. Yet an existence without sense experience, if conceivable at all, would be very poor and limited compared to what we enjoy now. Worse yet, we wouldn't have a brain, a fact which would apparently render all experience impossible. Nor can we conceive of ourselves as existing somehow in spite of this difficulty about experience. What could we be in a Next World without bodies? Without bodies we could not be extended in space. We would be non-spatial beings, if that is conceivable. But if we were not in space, would it make any sense to say that the next world is a spatial world? Apparently not. But if it were non-spatial it would be nowhere. And if we concede that it is nowhere, isn't that equivalent to saying that it simply doesn't exist at all?

Suppose, on the other hand, we try to conceive of ourselves as having a special sort of body—an "etheric," "spiritual," or "astral" body. Such a body would presumably have shape and size, and thus the world it inhabited would also have spatial dimensions and location in space. But if so, where would it be? In the constellation of Orion? In some other galaxy? Is it something that we could possibly journey to in our space travels? Somehow this line of inquiry seems profoundly mistaken, resembling an inquiry about the whereabouts of the Land of Oz. But even if this problem about the location of such a world could be resolved, there is an additional problem. Could we possibly remain one and the same person for very long if our new body and environment were radically different from the material body and environment of this world? It would seem not. If we were to suddenly find ourselves in a radically different body and environment (say, that of a fish in the ocean) with radically different needs and abilities, it is certain that we could not remain one and the same person over long periods of time in the way we presently do.

As a final closing of the door on the possibility of survival, one might argue that the distinction between a person and his physical body is illegitimate to begin with. Persons do not possess a physical body as they may possess a house or an automobile. Persons *are* physical beings. Since death is the destruction of the physical being whom we knew as a person, we must simply admit that it constitutes the destruction of the person. Even if something did survive this event, it couldn't be the person and thus wouldn't serve as evidence for personal survival.

If belief in survival is as radically mistaken as the above arguments suggest, why should it have arisen in the first place and then become widespread? Again, the skeptic of survival has a ready reply. Our hopes and our fears have a profound effect upon our judgment in these matters. Many people hope that death will result in a reunion with loved ones who have died. It is very difficult for them to accept the claim that they will *never again* be with those whom they dearly love. Others whose lives have been painful, limited, and frustrating may hope that a life after death will provide opportunities that they missed here. Some may hope for the continued opportunity to grow in knowledge and skill, or to go on making significant achievements. Then, too, there is the hope that there is a Next World in which justice is dispensed more equitably—where the good and the just shall finally receive their reward, and where injustice does not go unrecognized and unanswered.

Coupled with these various hopes, there is the fear, which becomes overpowering in some, that death constitutes the complete destruction of one's person—the fear that one shall be obliterated from the universe, never again to see the light of day, or to experience color, sound, joy, or anything whatsoever. We conceive of time as analagous to a line extending infinitely far into the past and future, and of our lifetimes as small segments on that line. Each individual event on the timeline occurs just once and is thus unique and unrepeatable. So it is with our lifetimes. With the moment of death one's time has elapsed, though time itself continues for all eternity. With this understanding, the prospect of ''never again'' is inescapable. We find ourselves thinking of time flowing on relentlessly without end, and of ourselves as out of existence, completely oblivious to it all. Such a prospect is terrible to some and at least unsettling to most of us. And since we find in ourselves an impulse to believe that which we hope is true and to repress that which we find fearful or terrible, it is easy to understand, so the argument goes, why the belief in a life after death is widespread even though devoid of factual or logical support.

These, then, are the main arguments which can be leveled against the belief in a life after death. They constitute a formidable group, and, after hearing them, there is a strong temptation to suppose that the issue is already settled. Nevertheless, I shall try to show that they are far from conclusive. I shall attempt to show, in the case of each, that it is mistaken and that it owes its apparent force to its agreement with a world view which, although seeming very plausible and even obviously true, is in error in many if not all of its aspects. This world view, which we may call the view of common sense, is not very well worked out and has ill-defined boundaries, but can be roughly characterized as consisting largely of uncritically acquired and unreflectively held beliefs concerning the nature of the world which are accepted as obviously true by the majority without question.

3

THE NATURE OF THE SELF

WHEN WE RAISE THE QUESTION OF WHETHER WE shall survive death it becomes obvious that the answer depends upon what we discover ourselves to be. Our ability to survive depends upon our nature. And when we inquire into our own nature, two features immediately come to mind: (1) that we have bodies and (2) that we are significantly more than our bodies. If we had discovered the human being to be nothing more than the physical creature that we apprehend with our senses, then there would be nothing mysterious about death. We would then know what death is. It would simply be the irreparable breakdown of the physical body, comparable to the breakdown of a complicated machine. The body breaks down into its component elements and the parts disperse, with many of them ending up in other living things. If the person were nothing more than this body which dies and decays, then the philosopher should turn his attention elsewhere; for death would be no mystery. But there is something more—there is mind or consciousness. It seems obvious that consciousness or awareness is quite different from the physical body and its activities. As you

13

read these words you become aware of what I am trying to communicate. You can directly apprehend the fact that you are aware and thus your awareness or consciousness must be a reality of some kind. But it seems to be a reality quite distinct from the activity or posture of your body.

The view that we have minds as well as bodies and that they are different things is in agreement with common sense. Commonsensically, we say such things as ''He has the body of an athlete'' and ''He has an analytical mind.'' But if we are to see if this view has any significance with respect to the question of life after death, we must take a careful look at our concepts of mind and body, of the mental and the physical. Perhaps the best approach is to note how the terms ''mental'' and ''physical'' are used. What things do we call mental and what do we term physical or material? The answer to the second question seems obvious: plants, rocks, stars, planets, clouds, brains, animal bodies, buildings, machines, and the like are physical. In addition to being located in space and occupying space, these things are publicly observable, i.e., they are perceivable by more than one person. More comprehensively, they are the substances, characteristics, events and processes which are apprehendable via the sense organs of more than one person. This is not to suggest that every physical object has been actually perceived. Some are hidden, some too far away, and some too small to be seen with the naked eye. There is a difference between being perceived and being perceivable. If the public perception of an object is possible, in the sense that we know what it would be like to perceive it, then we regard it as physical even if it has never been perceived.

We have just described the original and fundamental meaning of the term 'physical.' But it has another sense also. It is sometimes used to refer to the minute, unperceivable constituents of the physical things that we have been discussing. Physicists speak of atoms, waves, force-fields, and sub-atomic particles such as protons, positrons, neutrons, mesons, and electrons as material, and as composing the physical things that we sense. The minute constituents are in space even though they cannot be perceived. Their existence is merely inferred since they cannot be directly observed. But, it is argued, their existence *must* be inferred in order to account for the existence, nature, and behavior of the objects that we do perceive.

The term "mental" is used to refer to states of consciousness (or awareness) of various kinds. Thinking, believing, remembering, willing, wondering, desiring, sensing, and imagining are ways of being conscious. Since in states of consciousness we are always conscious of something, we must distinguish the consciousness itself from that something which we are being conscious of. In the case of, say, being conscious of the book on the table, the consciousness of the book being there must be distinguished from the fact that the book is on the table; for the book could be on the table without anyone being conscious of that fact. In other words, the act of consciousness must be distinguished from the object of consciousness. Since the object of consciousness can be anything, mental or physical, it is the act of consciousness that we must examine in order to discover the nature of the mental.

Consider your consciousness of what I have just been describing. You cannot deny that you are conscious of it (or conscious of something), for you can directly apprehend your own act of consciousness. Thus your consciousness must exist—its reality cannot be denied. But what is its nature, what features do all acts of consciousness have or fail to have? Perhaps the easiest point to note is that consciousness is not perceivable, i.e., not apprehendable via any of the sense organs. You can't see it, hear it, touch it, smell it or taste it. Suppose you are now sitting on or seeing a chair and are conscious of that chair. You can describe the chair in terms of its sense properties (its shape, size, color, solidity or hardness), but it is absurd to talk about your *consciousness* of the chair as rectangular or blue or hard or heavy. Not only is consciousness unperceived, it is unperceivable—we do not even know what it would be like to perceive it. In this respect it is radically different from the physical objects of our everyday experience.

The fact that consciousness is not perceivable certainly does not imply that it is not observable in any fashion. Perception is one means of observing the world, but not the only one. Though consciousness cannot be perceived, it can be observed so directly, immediately, and conclusively that its existence is, as we shall see, the most securely established in the world. It can be observed by means of a process which has been called "introspection," a fact which leads us to what is, perhaps, the salient feature of consciousness—its privacy. Though an act of consciousness is observable, it is only *privately* observable, that is to say, directly observable only by the person whose act it is. No one else can observe my act of consciousness in the direct way that I do. This is not to suggest that no one else can come to know about my act of consciousness. I may talk about it, describe it, or provide some other sign which reveals its presence. But these ways of knowing will necessarily be indirect compared with my direct access to my own conscious states.

Another way of expressing this matter is to assert that I have a privileged access to my own conscious state. You have to wait until you hear what I say, or read what I write, or observe my facial expressions to know what I am thinking about. But I do not! I have a direct, immediate access to my own states of mind which no one else has. Fortunately, I can introspectively observe my thoughts and subject them to critical evaluation before expressing them. Or, more generally, each person has a privileged access to his own conscious states which he does not have with respect to any physical object. Thus the privacy of conscious states must be taken as another feature rendering them different from physical things.

As we further examine our states of consciousness, we note that consciousness is always a consciousness *of* something or other. We are not simply conscious without being conscious of anything. An act of consciousness always has an object—that which the consciousness is *of* or *about*. The object of consciousness may be a physical thing, event, or process, or it may be an act of consciousness, as when we are conscious of our own consciousness. This "aboutness" character of consciousness is unique and serves as another basis for distinguishing consciousness from the physical. Physical things such as trees and tables are not *about* anything—they simply exist. Another way to put this very important point is to say that whereas consciousness is always a *consciousness* of something, physical things are neither *of* something nor *conscious* of anything. It might be argued that some words (e.g., nouns) are "about" the things they name, but it is obvious that whatever "aboutness" is involved in such cases has its source in the acts of consciousness which relate the word and the thing.

A final point which an examination of consciousness reveals is that it is not possible to locate consciousness as one can locate physical objects. We can introspect and observe that we are conscious, but we do not observe our consciousness to be in any particular place. We are tempted to say that our consciousness is in our head, but we certainly do not observe it to be there. Indeed, we do not even know what it would be like to find it in the brain. Suppose that someone (say, Jones) is aware of the bouquet of flowers on the table while a neuro-physiologist is examining the contents and activity of his brain. The neurophysiologist will certainly not find Jones' awareness of the flowers. He will not even find an image of a bouquet of flowers, although he would at least know what it would be like to find that. All he will find is blood, tissue, nerve cells and electrochemical activity.

The question as to where our consciousness is does not admit of an answer, not because we simply do not know where it is, but because it does not have a "where," i.e., it does not have spatial location. Nor does it have spatial extension. It may seem incredible that something should exist (as consciousness obviously does) and yet *not be anywhere*. But a closer look at the manner in which we come to know about consciousness will show that its non-spatial character is not surprising. We come to know that we are conscious by observing our consciousness, but without being able to perceive it. We observe it to be a reality that we cannot perceive, not because our sense organs are not keen enough, but because they run, so to speak, on a different track. We cannot even imagine what it would be like to apprehend consciousness with the sense organs. But it is through perception that we get our idea of spatiality. Perceivable entities are those that are located and extended in space. One might say that space is the form of perception, the form in which perception is construed. Thus it is not surprising that a reality which is observed but not perceived would not be observed as being in space.

The view that our minds are radically different in nature from our bodies and other physical things has been held by some of the most distinguished thinkers of the past. It was held by such intellectual giants as Plato, Kant, and Descartes. Descartes' view is of particular interest in this context. He held that the mind is a thing or substance. Body is also a substance. It is characteristic of a substance to exist by itself alone. Although God creates substance and sustains it in existence, it exists in itself alone in that we can form a clear conception of it without going beyond what we take it to be in itself. Upon forming such a conception, we find the essence of body to be extension in space, whereas the essence of mind is thought, and this is not extended or located in space.

Though it may have been established that mind and body are different things, we may yet wonder which is more intimately related to our being as selves. Is the self a physical being which has a mind, or is it a conscious being which is intimately connected with a body? Is the self essentially physical or essentially non-physical? Descartes advances an ingenious argument for thinking that the latter is the case. Descartes is very much concerned to attain absolute certainty in philosophy and observes that one can achieve this by discovering a claim or proposition which cannot be rendered doubtful even by the most radical doubt—a proposition so certain, so self-evident that its falsehood would be unthinkable. In order to generate the most radical doubt possible, Descartes entertains the supposition that there is an evil demon who is all-powerful and who is exercising all his power and ingenuity in attempting to deceive him. Descartes does not really believe in the existence of such a demon. Although he would acknowledge the possibility, his intent is to use the hypothesis that there is one to find a truth so basic that it is absolutely indubitable. He wants to use this hypothesis to order his beliefs in terms of their certainty.

Descartes begins his search for the indubitable truth by exposing his most basic beliefs to this radical doubt in an effort to see if they will remain unshaken by it. Many of these beliefs are based on what his senses reveal to him—that he has a physical body, that he is surrounded by a world of physical objects and other people, and that he is now seated in a chair in front of the fireplace writing the *Meditations*.[1] These beliefs seem so obviously true. Can they be shaken by any doubt? Descartes' conclusion is that they can. An all-powerful evil demon could generate a clever world of make-believe, a fictitious world of images similar to the dream world and cause Descartes to falsely believe that he is participating in a world of real physical objects and events. This deception may extend even to his own body. What he takes to be his physical body may in reality be a set of visual and tactile images generated by the demon and similar to the body he identified with in his dreams. Even simply mathematical truths are upset. Perhaps the demon causes him to make a mistake every time he tries to add or count or multiply.

Is there any belief so well-founded that the evil demon hypothesis does not upset it? Is any knowledge possible if we are subject to the deception of powers far beyond our comprehension? It would seem that all our beliefs, no matter how fundamental, must possess a measure of uncertainty to the extent that such a being is possible. It would seem so until Descartes directs his attention to the thinker himself, to the being immersed in doubt, and observes that although the thinker may be deceived about everything else, he cannot be deceived about his own existence. Regardless of the extent of the deception, he cannot be deceived about the fact that he exists; for he must *be* in existence in order to *be deceived*. He can doubt everything except his own existence. For he must exist in order to think, to doubt, to be deceived. His nonexistence is absolutely inconceivable while he is engaged in conceiving. Thus Descartes arrives at the absolutely indubitable truth which not even the most radical doubt can upset, and expresses it in his famous dictim, *Cogito, ergo sum*—I think, therefore I am.

We might wonder, however, about the significance of this truth, indubitable as it is. Although Descartes cannot doubt his existence he has done nothing about his doubt that he has a physical body, that he is in contact with an objective physical world, and that he has mathematical knowledge. If he cannot show that he has a physical body or that two plus two equals four, then what has he done? It is tempting to say "nothing at all," but this would surely be mistaken. For in demonstrating that he exists, at least as a thinking, conscious being, he has shown that our knowledge of our own consciousness is absolutely indubitable. We cannot doubt that we are conscious. Thinking and doubting are modes of consciousness and thus imply the existence of the conscious being engaged in these activities. Though we may be deceived about everything else, we cannot be deceived about our existence, at least as conscious beings. What Descartes has shown is that our knowledge of our existence as conscious beings is far more certain than our knowledge of anything physical.

It may now be apparent how Descartes' argument can be used to show not only that our knowledge of the existence of mind or consciousness is absolutely indubitable, but that mind is distinct from body and that the self is to be identified with the conscious being rather than the physical body. Descartes' argument can be construed as a demonstration of the existence of mind or consciousness. Since thinking, doubting, knowing, and wondering are mental processes, the existence of mind is not subject to doubt. And though the mind may be totally dependent on the body, it cannot be identical with the body. For if they were identical, then a demonstration of the existence of the mind would be equivalent to a demonstration of the existence of the body. But it is clear there is no such equivalence. The full force of Descartes' argument goes against it. He is consistently able to affirm his existence as a conscious or mental being while continuing to wonder whether he has a body. One might pull this point in the following way: If Descartes can doubt that he has a body, but cannot doubt that he exists, then what he is (his self) must be distinct from the physical body whose existence he is doubting. In other words, if one can at any given moment doubt the existence of X (the body) but cannot doubt the existence of Y (the self), then X and Y must be different things; for it is impossible to doubt and yet not doubt the existence of one and the same thing at one and the same time.

It will be worthwhile to examine even more carefully the relation between consciousness, mind, and self, since the possibility of the self surviving death depends so heavily upon the nature of the self. Are we simply using different words to refer to one and the same reality, or must we make some distinctions? We have taken a careful look at the nature of consciousness and have argued that the self is a non-physical conscious being. Though consciousness and the mind are very intimately related and are often not distinguished, I suggest that we regard the mind as being constituted, in part, by conscious states of the various kinds. My mind includes the conscious state I am having now, those I have had in the past, and those I will have in the future. But how is the self related to the mind? Am I simply a set or bundle of conscious states, or am I something more than that, viz., a being who *has* these conscious states in a most intimate way? The former view, which has been called the non-substantial view of the self, has some notable advocates. David Hume, the great Scottish philosopher, argues that the self as a being which has conscious states is not to be found in experience. All one finds are the various states of consciousness and, of course, what one is being conscious of. In a very famous passage Hume writes, "There are some philosophers, who imagine we are every moment intimately conscious of what we call our Self; that we feel its existence and its continuance in existence. . . . For my part, when I enter most intimately into what I call *myself*, I always stumble on some particular perception or other, of heat or cold, light or shade, love or hatred, pain or pleasure. I never can catch *myself* at any time without a perception, and never can observe any thing but the perception."[2]

We can observe the outward scene, and we can observe our various conscious states and how they affect one another. But we cannot observe ourselves engaged in the act of observing the outward scene or in the act of observing our own conscious states. When we "turn into" ourselves to look for the self in any way akin to the way we view chairs or landscapes, we, of course, find nothing. We seem to arrive at the same result when we try to observe the self in the way that we observe our own states of consciousness. The self simply does not appear as an object of consciousness. And we have no reason to assume the existence of that which does not appear in some way. Thus Hume is led to the conclusion that there is only the passing scene of experience—that the self is merely the bundle of experiences.

However acute Hume was in his observations, there is something quite unsatisfying about this account. For we find our experience to be unified in such a way that each of us is able to apprehend his own experience as the experience of a single self. Our ability to make sense out of our experience depends upon this. But it is difficult to see how a mere bundle of experiences could possess the necessary unity. Hume tries to account for the unity that we find in terms of certain relations or connections (such as resemblance, causation, and memory) which hold among the experiences themselves. But can such relations obtaining among otherwise discrete items account for the continuity that we find? Can they be used to explain why the experiences are organized around a center or apprehended as presented to one and the same subject? It would seem not. The unity of experience implies the existence of something which is present to each experience as it comes. There must be someone or something at the center of experience holding the various items of the bundle together in one consciousness.

This is the conclusion reached by Immanuel Kant, the great German philosopher. He agrees with Hume that when we try to find the self as an object of consciousness

we are unsuccessful. But the correct conclusion is not
that the self is nothing more than a bundle of experiences. Something more must be presupposed in order to
account for the unity and the organization that we find in
our experience. This something more cannot be identified with the items which it holds together in consciousness. Nor can it be known as they are known, for it
cannot be rendered as one more object of consciousness.
Yet the existence of this organizing, unifying entity must
be inferred in order to account for the nature of our experience (and thus can be indirectly known).

It appears, then, that the bundle view is inadequate.
Something in addition to the bundle is needed to make
possible the unification of experience. But can anything
else be known about this entity, this unifying subject of
experience? And can we have any direct, non-inferential
knowledge about it? Many influential thinkers have argued that we cannot. And perhaps they are right. The
subject of experience would somehow have to cease to
be the subject and become the object of experience which
is directly known. Yet it would have to remain the subject
to apprehend any object. Clearly, it cannot do both. It
would seem that it cannot be known at all, even indirectly, apart from some object of knowledge.

Though this argument seems to be a plausible one, it
is rendered suspect by its implication that the self as
subject of experience turns out to be a mysterious entity.
And this seems to be radically mistaken. It is certainly
tempting to assert that the self is not only not mysterious
but is in fact the reality that we know best. We are selves,
and there is surely a sense in which we know what we
are. But what we know cannot be described or characterized as we might describe any other object of knowledge, because we know the self in the very special way
of *being* it. And we simply don't know anything else in
that way. Though we know very well what it is to be
ourselves in the process of being aware of the world and

of our own conscious states, this knowledge is very difficult to recognize and assess. Perhaps the difficulty is due to the fact that such knowledge is absolutely unique. H.D. Lewis puts this elusive point well: ''At a certain level there is a lot that we do not know about ourselves. . . . But the way a person knows himself and his experiences initially is not mysterious in itself except in the sense that there is no further way in which it may be characterized. We do not know ourselves at this point by observation, or by anything resembling observation. There is nothing we detect in a way we can then point out or locate or describe, and the difficulty is that we are so accustomed, we might say almost conditioned, to learn about things by looking for them that we will persist, in the manner of Hume and in a way Locke before him, in 'turning into' ourselves to *look* for the self or observe and identify it and then of course find nothing.''[3]

The self is real but it is known as real in a manner that is inseparable from having some particular experience. Thus a careful examination of the relation between the self and its experience or conscious states may reveal more clearly the very special but elusive knowledge we have of it. The self cannot exist apart from conscious states. And conscious states cannot exist without belonging to a self. There is within the state of consciousness itself some kind of belonging or being the experience of some being. It is presented to a being as a state of that being. This belonging is not a verbal matter or a matter of convention. It is given and ultimate. It is what one simply finds experience as such to involve.

In the very act of having a conscious state, I am aware of it as being uniquely my experience. It is certainly not simply something that happens and which can be shown in some further way to belong to me. I do not, for example, have a thought and then discover that it is mine. There is no intervening stage between having a thought and experiencing it as belonging to me. It belongs to me in the very special way in which thoughts are had. It is uniquely mine, but the way in which it is cannot be indicated other than to say that it belongs to me in a way familiar to all of us—the way in which we have thoughts and sensations. There is no completely adequate term for what we find to be the case here. But perhaps we can do quite well without one. Each of us is familiar with the kind of belonging in question, for it is apparent in having experience of any kind. What it means for an experience to belong to a self is evident enough in itself. It is elusive only in the sense that nothing further can be said about it.

It is becoming apparent that the relation between the self and its experience is of a very special sort. I am not related to my experiences in the way I am related to external things or the way in which external things are related to each other. My experience is involved in an essential way in what I find myself to be in having any experience—not a being apart from and confronting my experiences, but involved in having the experience and known, even to me, only by having it. Yet I am more than this experience, although no indication of this "more" can be given beyond the awareness of it that each of us has from his own case in having any experience.

We are now in a position to evaluate some of the previously mentioned arguments which were supposed to show that survival of death is impossible. Consider the arguments that man is a completely material being and that death simply constitutes the total destruction of that being. These materialistic views range from the rather crude position of the 18th-century physiologist, Cabanis, who held that thought is nothing but a secretion of the brain, to the sophisticated modern mind-brain identity theory. But I have argued that consciousness—the principle component of mind—is undeniably real and that an observation of its nature reveals it to be radically different from the brain or any other physical thing. The brain is a good example of a physical thing. It has spatial location and is extended in space. It has color, shape, size, and mass. It can be observed by more than one person and, unlike consciousness, is not about anything. As Congdon rather amusingly describes it, "It can be painted green or thrown at a wall or hung up to dry."[4] But none of this is true of consciousness. Suppose I were to assert that my awareness of what I am writing now is blue, or that my thought of my grandmother is triangular and weighs two pounds, or that my idea of an elephant is larger than my idea of a mouse. The absurdity of such assertions points to the radical difference between consciousness and the brain.

Perhaps a bit more attention should be given to the mind-brain identity theory since it seems to be the most attractive of the various materialistic views. It is espoused by many contemporary philosophers. According to the identity theory, states of consciousness are identical with (i.e., one and the same as) certain brain states. They are one and the same reality known in different ways. What is experienced subjectively as, say, the awareness of a red patch is objectively an activity taking place in one's brain. But how are we to understand the assertion that they are one and the same? In the very process of trying to understand how the thing which has the characteristic of being my awareness of a red patch can be one and the same as the thing which has the characteristic of being an activity in my brain, it becomes apparent that, irrespective of whether these *things* can be identified, there are two different *characteristics* involved. That the characteristics, at least, are different is difficult to deny. For, as C.D. Broad points out:

There are some questions which can be raised about the characteristic of being a molecular movement, which it is nonsensical to raise about the characteristic of being an awareness of a red patch; and conversely. About a molecular movement it is perfectly reasonable to raise the question: Is it swift or slow, straight or circular, and so on? About the awareness of a red patch it is nonsensical to ask whether it is a swift or a slow awareness, a straight or a circular awareness, and so on. Conversely, it is reasonable to ask about an awareness of a red patch whether it is a clear or a confused awareness; but it is nonsense to ask of a molecular movement whether it is a clear or a confused movement. Thus the attempt to argue that "being a sensation of so and so" and "being a bit of bodily behavior of such and such a kind" are just two names for the same characteristic is evidently hopeless.[5]

An identity theorist may try to defend his view by claiming that although the phrase "my awareness of a red patch" does not have the same *meaning* as the phrase "a brain process," these phrases nevertheless *refer* to one and the same reality. He would probably add that the fact that the term "lightning" does not mean the same as "electrical discharge" does not prevent these terms from referring to one and the same event. Lightning is in fact an electrical discharge, and, similarly, a state of awareness is in fact a brain process.

However, this line of argument will not do. If an act of awareness and a brain process are one and the same, then every characteristic of the one must also be a characteristic of the other. But, as we have seen, an act of awareness has characteristics that the physical does not have, and vice versa. For example, a brain process has the characteristic of being located in the place where the brain is, but this is not true of conscious states. We give location to pain and other bodily sensations, but these sensations must be distinguished from our awareness of them. Though I may locate the pain as being in

my shoulder, it makes no sense to say that my awareness of this pain is also in my shoulder. Nor does it
make any sense to say that my awareness of the pain is
in my brain, for I do not even know what it would be
to find it there.

Now, if it makes no sense to speak of my conscious
states as taking place in the space occupied by my brain,
then the identity theory must be mistaken. For a necessary condition that something must meet if it is identical
with a physical object, event, or process is that it must
be in the place where the latter is. If it is *not* there, then
it cannot be identical with what *is* there. Thus states of
consciousness and brain processes cannot be one and the
same.

It is true that I have described consciousness mainly
by a process of negation—it is not perceivable, it is not
extended, it does not have spatial location. And it may
seem that this renders the existence of consciousness
suspect, since the same could be said about nothing.
But consciousness is certainly not nothing! We have direct experience of it, and thus have the best possible
grounds for asserting its existence. We do not doubt that
the world contains blue objects because we see them.
Similarly, we ought not doubt that consciousness is real
because we observe that as well. Indeed, as we have
seen, since we are conscious beings, our knowledge that
consciousness exists (and that the self exists) has certainty that we cannot hope to achieve with respect to
anything else.

Though the existence of consciousness as a non-physical
reality does negate the various materialistic views of the
nature of man, it certainly does not imply that we shall
not be destroyed by death. For it may be that the existence of consciousness is dependent upon the brain and
body. In that case, the death of the body will entail the
cessation of consciousness and, consequently, the de-

struction of the person. Thus the mystery of death boils down to the question of what happens to consciousness when the brain dies. Our concern is one about the destiny of our consciousness.

4

THE ROLE OF THE BODY

THE VIEW OF THE SELF FOR WHICH I HAVE BEEN AR-
guing, viz., that the self is essentially a conscious being
or subject of consciousness rather than a physical organism, may be difficult for many to accept. It may seem
that I have not sufficiently recognized the importance of
the body with respect to the question of the nature of the
self. I have already spoken of various ways in which body
and, particularly, brain states affect consciousness. Blows
to the head, brain damage, fatigue, illness, and drugs, to
name a few, have an undeniable, and sometimes profound, effect on consciousness.

But the body is rather intimately involved in our
experience in other ways which have not yet been discussed. The activity of the sense organs in conjunction
with the location and posture of the body ordinarily determines the perceptual experience that we have. Our
perceptions change from moment to moment as a movement in the location or posture of the body alters our
perspective. Moreover, we have the experience of doing
the perceiving from a "point of view" which coincides
with the position of the body.

The sense of touch along with the sensitivity of various parts of the body are involved in a very important way in a significant portion of our experience. As I reach out and touch something with my finger, not only do I have a sensation and find my awareness is thereby affected, but the tactile sensation seems to be located in my finger. If I stumble against the table, the sensation seems to be where my body and the table come into contact. From time to time I feel pain in some part of my body, and I can generally give this a rather precise location. And then there are those bodily sensations which I seem to feel continuously but more vaguely from within than on the surface of my body. There can be no doubt that such sensations do much to generate the impression that I almost am my body in some respects.

Another source of this impression is the fact that we can express ourselves and have an effect upon the world only through our bodies. We can conceive of a world which is different in these respects—one in which objects at a distance respond merely to my desire without my having to move them with my body, and in which other people seem to know about my thoughts and feelings without my having to express them. But in our actual world, except for the possibility of rare cases of paranormal functioning (such as telepathy and psychokinesis), this is not the case. Our effect upon the external world is limited by what we can do through our bodies. Since all of our contact with the world is mediated through our bodies, we come to speak of them and apparently regard them as simply being ourselves. They are ourselves in operation. Thus it is not surprising that we are led to feel, if mistakenly, that we are one with our bodies.

Because we communicate our thoughts and emotions so spontaneously and so effortlessly by way of our bodies, there is a temptation to suppose that we are directly observing the mental states of another when we observe his body. Facial expressions, gestures, tones of voice, and a great variety of bodily activities reveal our mental states so readily and so constantly that it is easy to slip into identifying our inner states with this continual and spontaneous expression of them. When we are angry we shout or scowl, and when sad we look dejected. Although we can conceal our inner states, it is normally the case that our bodies mirror our minds in such an intricate and accurate manner, that it may seem that our very souls are bared to the outside world. Thus we come to suppose that when people observe the various activities of our bodies they are looking at ourselves, and, consequently, we are again tempted to identify ourselves with our bodies. But it is clear that we must distinguish our inner states from the behavioral manifestation of them. The shout or the scowl is not the anger that we experience, nor is the dejected look—the drawn face or drooping shoulders—the sadness that we feel. And the pensive look is not the thought itself. We do not actually *perceive* the sadness or the conscious states of another, however carefully we listen to what he says about them, or however carefully we observe his gestures, facial expressions, and other visible indicators. Our conscious states themselves are not directly observed by another, however accurately, effortlessly, and spontaneously our bodies express them.

No one can deny that such facts demonstrate the intimate relationship between the self and the body. It is far more intimate than, say, the relationship between an automobile and its driver. But they fail to show that the self and the body are identical. A consideration of the role of the body in perception shows that our awareness of the world is profoundly affected by, indeed, *made possible by*, the body. The fact that we can act on the world only through the body gives rise to countless tactile and somatic sensations which constitute an important part of our experience. And, finally, it seems that all experience, all conscious activity whatsoever, is a function of a specific part of the body, namely, the brain. But however profoundly the body affects consciousness and however extensively it may even *generate* awareness, the fact remains that consciousness cannot be one and the same as the brain or body. It is certainly the case that one thing can casually affect another without those things being one and the same. A draft can be the cause of a head cold without a draft and a head cold being one and the same thing. Thus it is entirely consistent with these facts to maintain that the self is a conscious being, a non-physical subject of consciousness intimately connected with and deeply affected by its body.

Yet it may seem that there is one matter raised in this discussion of the role of the body which still constitutes a problem for the view that the self is non-physical. It concerns the fact that tactile sensations, pains, and the continuously felt bodily sensations are in space and felt to be located in the body. For if feeling aches, pains, tickles, and the like are mental processes, then some mental realities are extended in space and located in the body. And thus it may seem that even if the self is of the nature of mind, i.e., a conscious being, it is not distinct from the body. But when the proper distinctions are made, it will be seen that these sensations do not provide evidence for such a conclusion.

Many philosophers regard such sensations as mental, probably because they are only privately apprehendable. And, as we have seen, privacy is not a feature of physical things as they are commonly understood. But even if such sensations are regarded as mental, they must nevertheless be distinguished from acts of awareness or what we might now call the "strictly mental." For acts of awareness (i.e., acts of consciousness) are, as we have seen, non-spatial, non-perceivable, and have the feature of "aboutness," in addition to their privacy. Thus they are very different from sensations of pain and touch. Perhaps the most important difference relevant to this discussion is that acts of awareness are inextricably bound up with the nature of the self in a way that pains and tactile sensations are not. Aches, pains, and tactile sensations do not seem necessary to the existence of the self. I understand that there are people who have little or no capacity for tactile sensations. At any rate I can conceive of myself not having such feeling in my body almost as easily as I can reflect upon the fact that I do not have feeling in anyone else's body. But consciousness, as we have seen, *is* necessary to the existence of the self.

The ambiguity of the word "sensation" is a source of confusion in this matter. We could use the word "sensation" to mean (1) the mental activity of sensing something, or (2) what is sensed. A case of sensing or seeing a chair, for example, can be analyzed into two parts: (1) the mental activity of seeing the chair, and (2) the chair which is seen. Since seeing is a way of being aware, we must distinguish between our awareness of the chair and the chair we are aware of. But feeling is also a way of being aware. Awareness is involved in feeling tickles, itches, hunger pangs, and the experience of touching and being touched. But these feelings must, as objects of our awareness, be distinguished from our awareness of them. Pains, for example, are distinguishable from our awareness of them. And once this distinction is acknowledged, there will be no inclination to regard pain as "strictly mental."

Though pains and tactile sensations are not "strictly mental," they are not physical either, as that term is commonly understood. For they can be directly experienced only by the person who has them, and they exist only so long as they are being experienced. In other words, they are private and mind-dependent. Thus it seems that there are realities which are neither strictly mental nor physical. Pains and tactile sensations are not the only members of this class. Also included are after-images, memory images, hallucinations and dream imagery. They are not strictly mental, for they are not acts of awareness. Moreover, they are extended in space (though not in physical space),[1] and they are perceivable. But they are not physical either, for they are private to the one who experiences them and exist only while they are being experienced.

It must be admitted that there are difficulties which remain in our understanding of the nature of pain, tactile sensations, and those bodily sensations which seem to be more within than on the surface of the body. Certainly there is a need for further investigation in this area. But the point to be noted is that they must be distinguished from our consciousness of them; for, unlike consciousness, they are not *of* or *about* anything.[2] Nor are they *conscious* of anything. Rather, they are phenomena which the self or subject becomes aware of, and, as such, belong to the object pole of the subject-object dichotomy. Furthermore, they seem to have extension and location in space. And, as we have seen, the very nature of consciousness is such that it cannot have spatial extension, however much it may inform us of extended things. So, however much our pains and bodily sensations, together with the fact that we perceive and communicate by means of our bodies, may incline us to identify ourselves with our bodies, it appears that these considerations do not serve as *grounds* for such an identification.

5

Is Consciousness Produced by the Brain?

Though states of consciousness and brain states are not identical, it is apparent that consciousness is a function of the brain. That is, consciousness varies with the state of the brain. This functional dependence of consciousness on the brain is dramatically apparent when brain activity is profoundly altered as in the case of brain lesions, surgical disconnection of portions of the brain, brain damage resulting from strokes, forceful blows to the head, and exposure to powerful hallucinogenic drugs. This dependence is the basis of some of the most persuasive arguments against thinking that we will survive bodily death. Such arguments (which were stated earlier) are especially convincing because they appear to be based upon abundant evidence which is readily observed and available to everyone. Each of us can observe in his own case the countless number of instances of apparent dependence of mind upon body, as, for example, in the case of fatigue, alcohol consumption, and illness.

Yet these arguments, powerful as they seem to be, are based upon an assumption which can and must be questioned. The assumption is that consciousness is the *prod-*

uct of the neural processes taking place in the brain. The brain produces consciousness, just as the teakettle produces steam and the electric current produces light. It generates consciousness in its interior, just as it generates various chemical substances and electrical phenomena. This is the assumption involved when one points to the effects of a blow on the head, although it is often unconsciously employed. What this assumption implies about survival is obvious—when the brain is destroyed, its productive function ceases, and thus consciousness must perish also.

But this assumption must be questioned. For the fact that all signs of consciousness cease when the brain is badly injured or destroyed does not *imply* that consciousness is a *product* of brain activity. It is surely conceivable that some relationship other than that of production would yield the same result. That is, if the relationship were of a different sort and consciousness were left intact, it would still not be surprising if all signs of consciousness were to cease. For it is obvious how important the body is for the manifestation of consciousness. If one should find himself still in existence after the death of his body, but now as a disembodied conscious being without physical sense organs or speech organs, he would find it impossible to make his existence known to us, at least in any normal fashion.

But what are the alternatives to supposing that consciousness is produced by the brain? It is true that nature provides abundant examples of what seem to be productive function. But it also provides examples of other kinds of function. The trigger of a rifle or of a crossbow, for example, has a releasing function. The crossbow trigger releases the bowstring and thus releases the energy in the bow. And we find what we might call transmissive function in the case of such things as prisms, lenses, and colored glass. They do not produce light but merely transmit it with some modification. So when we consider the fact that consciousness is a function of the brain, we are certainly entitled to consider kinds of function other than production.

We assume that consciousness is a product of brain activity because it varies with brain states, and all signs of it cease when the brain is severely injured. To see how much is being assumed, consider an analogous case: We are watching a television program when the television falls to the floor and smashes into pieces. Consequently, all signs of the existence of the television program cease. So we conclude that the television set must have been producing the program. Of course, we wouldn't draw that conclusion because we know that television sets do not function in this way. But it may be that when we draw such a conclusion about consciousness we are making a mistake of the very sort that we would be making if we were to conclude that the television set must have been producing the program.

Fantastic as this suggestion may seem at first glance, it may be that the brain functions more like a receiver or transmitter of consciousness than a producer of it. Perhaps some term such as "transceiver," "inhibitor," "selective transmitter," "reducing valve," or "detector" more accurately describes the relationship between consciousness and the brain than does "producer." The first point to note about this suggestion is that it is just as consistent with what we observe about the way consciousness varies with the state of the brain as the production theory. Any change in brain functioning, such as that resulting from a stroke or a blow to the head, could be expected to affect its capacity as a transceiver or detector just as certainly as its capacity as a producer. That we observe consciousness to vary with the state of the brain is precisely what we should expect if the brain did function as a transceiver or detector of consciousness.

This suggestion that the source of consciousness lies other than in the brain is one that deserves to be explored. Let us consider a way in which it can be conceived. "Suppose, for example," writes William James, "that the whole universe of material things—the furniture of earth and the choir of heaven—should turn out to be a mere surface-veil of phenomena, hiding and keeping back the world of genuine realities."[1] This notion that the world we observe is a world of mere appearance which must be distinguished from the world of reality is certainly not foreign to either eastern or western philosophical thought. One thinks of Kant's basic distinction between the phenomenal world that we apprehend and the real world of *noumena* which is utterly beyond our reach. Then there is the eastern doctrine of the world of *maya*, the veil-like world of appearance which hides the world of reality. Nor is this distinction foreign to common sense. As William James puts it, "Common sense believes in realities behind the veil even too superstitiously."[2]

Now, suppose that our brains have the unique function of serving as organs of communication between the two worlds in that they are, shall we say, thin spots in the veil through which consciousness from the real world is transmitted. The variation in degree of consciousness that we experience, from lucidity of thought when our minds are quick and teeming with ideas to the dullness of fatigue, depression, and illness, corresponds to a thinning and thickening of the semi-transparent spot in the veil which is the brain. Though our brains are the points of transaction between the two worlds they function as obstructions or filters impeding the flow of consciousness, sometimes severely as when damaged by a stroke or a lesion and sometimes minimally as during periods of alertness and lucidity of thought. As the obstruction to the transmission of consciousness varies, so does consciousness itself. And when the brain dies, the stream of consciousness which it transmitted would vanish from this world. But there is no reason to suppose that it could not remain intact and continue on in ways unknown to us.

Since this theory implies that the source of consciousness is independent of the brain, some conception of the source would make the theory much more complete. It would seem that there are two possibilities worth considering. Either there is a single cosmic consciousness or else there is a source of consciousness corresponding to each of us. Perhaps the experience of the mystic suggests the former. The mystic claims to have had an experience in which all distinctions, even that between subject and object of consciousness, disappear to yield a totally undifferentiated unity. Both self and world disappear into the unity. This unity seems to involve consciousness, but, the mystic claims, it is a radically different kind of consciousness—it is a consciousness which is not *of* anything. Now, if the source is a single consciousness, then, upon death, individuality as we know it would not be preserved. However, it may be that the loss of individuality need not be total. It is interesting to note that even though the mystic apparently experiences a loss of the sense of self as he blends with the world into the undifferentiated unity, he nevertheless remembers and regards the mystical experience as something that happened to *him* rather than to something impersonal. So the loss of individuality need not be regarded as any more complete than that experienced in the mystical state.

But suppose that there is a source of consciousness corresponding to each of us. On this alternative, individuality would be preserved, and, as we shall see, the preservation of individuality beyond death is suggested by various kinds of apparently paranormal phenomena cited later on in this book. Since the source would be in a world which transcends this one and is inaccessible to us, let us call the source which corresponds to me my "transcendental self." And let us call the self that I presently observe myself to be my "empirical self." On this view, my empirical self is my transcendental self as modified by the transmitting or filtering properties of my brain. Perhaps the relationship between them can be conceived as analogous to the relationship between myself awake and myself in a non-lucid dream state (i.e., a dream state in which I do not realize that I am dreaming and do not remember my waking life). It is obvious to me (though perhaps not describable in some further way) from the vantage point of my waking state that I am one and the same as the self who was in a non-lucid dream state. I remember the events of the dream as an episode in my conscious life. I remember them as having been presented to me, the being who is now doing the remembering. I know in a very basic sense what it is to be myself, and I remember myself in the dream as the being I now find myself to be. Though this establishes, in the most complete way possible, that I am one and the same being as the dreamer, it certainly does not entail that the dreamer is aware of this while dreaming.

Now, suppose that the empirical self is comparable to the dreamer. And suppose that the transmitting properties of the brain are such that the fundamental sense of what it is to be oneself—to be the subject of consciousness that is having this experience—gets through unmodified, but awareness of any transcendental episode is blocked. Then the death of the brain with the consequent elimination of the blockage would be comparable to awakening from a non-lucid dream. One would awaken to his transcendental self. This awakening would be experienced as consciousness expansion, comparable to the way, upon awakening, we find ourselves to be in an expanded state of consciousness which includes the dream awareness to which we were limited before awakening, plus a great deal more.

In this view, voluntary behavior would be explained not as the effect of the electrochemical activity of the brain on the body but as the transcendental self making an impact on the physical world through the mechanism of the brain. And perception would be explained not in terms of the brain generating perceptual experience in response to stimulation by the sense organs but as the result of the activity of the transcendental self using the brain and sense organs to attain consciousness of the physical world.

At this point a critic may respond by asserting that this hypothesis is nothing but a mixture of foolish metaphor and unbridled speculation. Maybe we can conceive of the brain transmitting consciousness instead of producing it. And maybe we can't point to any facts which we observe about the way consciousness varies with brain states which rule this out. We can't show that it is false, but is there any evidence for thinking that it is true? Isn't it much simpler and more plausible to suppose that the brain produces consciousness? Isn't consciousness really more comparable to steam or electricity which is produced on the spot in a teakettle or electrical generator, as the case may be? Isn't it more rigorously scientific to regard the brain as a producer of consciousness?

Admittedly, the theory of production is a popular theory. We assume its truth and think in terms of it, often without making our assumption explicit. Because we are familiar with it, we are inclined to regard it as the simpler, more plausible theory. Nevertheless, if we confine ourselves to what we strictly observe about the consciousness-brain relation, we shall find that the answer to these questions is "No." Strictly speaking, what the scientist observes is that consciousness and brain states vary concomitantly—when the brain activity changes in a certain way, then consciousness changes also. When there is activity in the temporal lobe consciousness hears things, when in the occipital lobe it sees things, and when in the lower frontal region it says things to itself. A change in the one occurs regularly in conjunction with a change in the other. This constant conjunction of two different things, this concomitant variation is all that the scientist ever observes. He never observes the activity in, say, the temporal lobes *producing* the experience of hearing. It is not even clear what it would be to observe that.

Of course, we may wonder why there is this concomitant variation. And then we are led to talk about production or transmission; for whether the brain were producing consciousness or transmitting it, it would be understandable that certain brain states and states of consciousness should regularly occur together in the way that we observe. But the point is that the production hypothesis, as well as the hypothesis of transmission, is something *added* to what we observe in order to account for our observation. Production, if it occurs at all, is something behind the scene, and thus we might call the production hypothesis a metaphysical one.

But even though we do not even observe the brain producing consciousness, and that, consequently, the view that production occurs must be regarded as a mere assumption or postulate, a defender of that view may still claim that it is more plausible than the transmission hypothesis. He may argue that the transmission theorist is unable to explain the details of transmission. How, he may ask, can the brain be an organ for selectively transmitting and modifying to a certain form a consciousness which has its source other than in the brain? But the defense against this attack is obvious—one need only point out that the defender of the production view can do no better. The exact details of either process are completely unknown. Science has nothing to offer here. How can the brain, a material substance, produce something as radically different from it as consciousness is? How can the brain create out of its own material substance a reality that has no mass, no shape, no size, and is not even in space? We seem to have some insight into the way heated water in a teakettle produces steam (provided that the notion of production is acceptable at all), for water and steam are merely different forms of the same substance. We add energy in the form of heat to the water molecules and excite them to the point where they evaporate into steam. We simply alter the molecular motion. But as far as our understanding goes of how the brain could create something as radically different from it as consciousness, we might just as well say that consciousness is created out of nothing. Thus the defender of the production view certainly doesn't get the better of this argument.

Even though the transmission view seems fantastic, at least to begin with, it turns out to be no less plausible and no less scientific than the production view. Perhaps this is because an examination of the production view reveals it to be rather fantastic. At any rate, there is no basis for preferring one over the other in what has been discussed so far. But there are some other considerations which seem to provide a basis for preferring the transmission view or a view which, unlike the production view, is compatible with survival of death.

One such consideration is the evidence for the claim that at least some people have survived bodily death and have managed to communicate that fact to the living. Since this is a matter that I will consider in detail at a later point, I will say no more about it here other than to note that the truth of such a claim would support not only the transmission view but also other views compatible with survival of death.

Another consideration has to do with the effect of certain drugs on the brain and on consciousness. In his book, *The Doors of Perception*,[3] Aldous Huxley describes and reflects upon his experiences under the influence of mescaline. On the basis of that experience he is led to a version of what I have called the selective transmission or inhibitory view of the function of the brain and nervous system. Huxley espouses and seems to accept the view that the function of the brain, nervous system, and sense organs is eliminative rather than productive in that they shut out most of what we would otherwise perceive or remember at any moment and leave only that very special selection which is likely to be biologically useful. He suggests that each of us is potentially "Mind at Large,"[4] capable of perceiving everything that is happening everywhere and of remembering everything that has happened to us. The brain and nervous system function as a "cerebral reducing valve," through which "Mind at Large" is funneled. Consciousness is thus reduced to that limited utilitarian portion which enables us to compete successfully in the struggle for survival.

Since most of us know only what comes through the reducing valve, we believe that reduced consciousness is the only consciousness. However, some people (viz., mystics, visionaries, and psychics) seem to be born with a kind of bypass around their reducing valve and others acquire a temporary one through the use of meditation, yoga, hypnosis, and certain drugs. Huxley suggests that mescaline is one such drug—a drug having the power to impair the efficiency of the cerebral reducing valve and thereby create a temporary bypass. He explains that mescaline inhibits the production of the enzymes which regulate the supply of glucose to the brain and thereby places the brain in a sugar-starved state. Though the intellect does not seem to be affected when the sugar supply is reduced, perception and volition are profoundly altered. Huxley tells us that perception, particularly visual perception, is enormously improved, but volition suffers a decline. Since one under the influence of mescaline has better things to think about, he cannot be motivated to do the things which at ordinary times he would consider important. Interest in space is reduced, as one is now primarily concerned with "being and meaning"[5] rather than distances and locations. And interest in time falls almost to zero.

Huxley now reveals how these facts support his view that the brain functions as a reducing valve:

These effects of mescaline are the sort of effects you could expect to follow the administration of a drug having the power to impair the efficiency of the cerebral reducing valve. When the brain runs out of sugar, the undernourished ego grows weak, can't be bothered to undertake the necessary chores, and loses all interest in those spatial and temporal relationships which mean so much to an organism bent on getting on in the world. As Mind at Large seeps past the no longer watertight valve, all kinds of biologically useless things start to happen. In some cases there may be extra-sensory perceptions. Other persons discover a world of visionary beauty. To others again is revealed the glory, the infinite value and meaningfulness of naked existence, of the given, unconceptualized event. In the final stage of egolessness there is an "obscure knowledge" that All is in all—that All is actually each. This is as near, I take it, as a finite mind can ever come to "perceiving everything that is happening everywhere in the universe."[6]

However, one might use these considerations to support the inhibitory view of brain functioning in a somewhat different way. Huxley suggests that he experienced a kind of consciousness expansion or enhancement as a result of the mescaline. His consciousness expands as Mind at Large seeps through his no longer impervious reducing valve. Now, if he is right about the way mescaline acts on the brain, then the effects that he experienced are certainly not what we might expect to result from the impairment of a consciousness *generator*. If the brain functions as a consciousness producer or generator, then it would seem that substances such as glucose and oxygen are the raw materials out of which it fashions its product. Reducing the supply of raw materials would result in a diminishment of the product. On the other hand, if the brain functions as a selective inhibitor of consciousness, such an interference in its operations would render it less efficient in its inhibitory function and thus provides a basis for expecting consciousness to be expanded or enhanced. Thus if Huxley experienced an enhancement of consciousness as a result of the mescaline, this fact would support the view that the brain is a selective inhibitor of consciousness.

Certain features of near-death experiences also support the selective-transmission view. People who were drowning or who have been on the brink of dying through some other extremely life-threatening situation often report having had extraordinary memories at the time. They report having experienced their entire lives flashing before their eyes with incredible rapidity. In his book entitled *Life After Life*,[7] Raymond Moody considers the cases of numerous people who had undergone clinical death and later returned to life. Instead of being unconscious while they were clinically dead, many found themselves having experiences which they were able to remember and describe. Several spoke of their vision and hearing (or something analogous to these senses) as becoming more perfect and of their thought becoming more lucid and more rapid.

Such phenomena certainly appear to go against the view that the brain produces consciousness. On the production view it would seem that consciousness and memory would grow dim when the brain is deprived of oxygen, as in the case of drowning. But extraordinary memory would not be surprising if the brain functioned as an inhibitor of memory, perhaps limiting memory to that which is, in the main, relevant to survival. Such a function is very compatible with the view (for which we have evidence acquired from experiments with hypnosis) that nothing is ever forgotten totally beyond recall. And when the brain is in great trouble, as it must be after clinical death has taken place, one would certainly not expect thought to become more lucid and more rapid if the brain were generating it.

Further support for the view that the brain does not function as a producer of consciousness derives from the painstaking efforts of contemporary neurologists and other scientists who have been studying brain structure and neural activity in the brain. It was once commonly assumed that there must be something very distinctive about the structure, chemical composition, or metabolic processes of the nerve cells in the brain. Thus McDougall, in 1911, asks, "What is there in the nature or the activities of these various structures to suggest that they can in some way produce or generate the unique phenomenon of consciousness?"[8] But now it is known that the nerve cell is surprisingly similar to all other cells in chemical composition and general structure. And their metabolic processes do not distinguish them either.

Not only is the nerve cell like other cells, but there are no essential differences between those nerve cells in the cortex which are sometimes involved with consciousness and those in the spinal cord which never are. Because of this, researchers expected to find a difference in the way the synapses between the cells are organized. But no such difference has been found. All synapses show a remarkable similarity, both in their essential structure and in the manner in which a nerve impulse is transmitted across them. Thus, to conclude as Burt does, "*it would seem impossible to suppose*, as so many physiologists used to do when all this was still wrapped in mystery, *that these very ordinary chemical processes can 'generate' anything like conscious experience.* . . . A comparison of the specific micro-neural situations in which consciousness does and does not arise suggests that the brain functions, not as a generator of consciousness, but rather as a two-way transmitter and detector."[9]

It seems justifiable to conclude, then, that the selective transmission view is as plausible as the production view and may be preferable to it.[10] However, it may be that neither is true and that we ought to look for something

better. We noted earlier that all we observe about the
relation between brain states and states of consciousness
is that they vary concomitantly. We do not observe either
production or selective transmission. Rather, such processes are postulated *to account for* the concomitant variation that we observe. But it is conceivable that the
concomitant variation does not stand in need of any account. It may be simply a brute fact about our world that
these two different kinds of things vary concomitantly—
a fundamental fact which neither admits of nor requires
any account.

Perhaps we can probe into this matter a little further
by raising the question as to what it is to account for
something. It seems that we account for the existence of
something by citing its cause or causes. We account for
a certain state of consciousness by referring to the brain
state which caused it. But, as David Hume pointed out
long ago, we never observe its cause to be anything more
than that with which it varies concomitantly. We do not,
for example, observe the cause producing the effect. We
are still entitled to speak of conscious states causing brain
states and vice versa, but we must realize that this is just
a shorthand way of referring to events that are constantly
conjoined. Thus to account for something is simply to
relate it to something else with which it varies concomitantly. And if this is the case, then we ought not suppose
that the constant conjunction of consciousness and brain
states that we observe must stand in need of some account. Or, more precisely, one can provide an account if
all that is meant is a more complete description of the
other things with which the fact being accounted for is
associated. But we need not suppose that there is an account involving a statement of the metaphysical source
of the constant conjunction.

We do ask *how* an event C causes another event E. This
is an intelligible question if we are asking about the intermediary causal steps through which C eventually

causes E. For example, our question of how the application of nitrogen fertilizer causes the grass to grow better can be answered by learning about the intermediary causal steps between the application of the nitrogen and the improved growth. When there are intermediary causal steps between the cause and the effect we shall call the causal sequence a case of *remote* causation. Since most causal sequences that we concern ourselves with are of this sort and since in the case of such sequences it makes sense to ask how the earlier event causes the later one, we suppose that such a question makes sense in the case of every causal sequence. But this may not be the case. For there are cases of *proximate* causation—cases in which no events intervene between cause and effect. And since the question of *how* a given event caused some other event may never have any meaning other than through what intermediary causal steps it was effected, it may be that in the case of proximate causation this "how" question loses the only meaning it ever has.

Now, the case of a conscious state and the brain state which corresponds to it is a case of proximate causation. Thus it may be that the question as to how the brain state causes the corresponding conscious state is misguided. It may be that it makes no sense to ask (i.e., that we do not know what we have in mind when we ask) how or why a brain state causes a state of consciousness or vice versa. But it seems that it is via the question of how or why one thing causes another that the idea of production creeps in. We assume that some further explanation of the consciousness-brain relation is possible and are tempted to suppose that production of the conscious state by the brain state is this further explanation. But if the question of how one thing causes another makes no sense at the level of proximate causation, then it would not make sense to claim that the consciousness-brain relation can be accounted for by supposing that one produces the other.

It may be, then, that the concomitant variation of conscious states and brain states is an ultimate fact about our world which does not stand in need of and does not admit of any metaphysical or non-empirical account. In other words, it may be that neither selective transmission nor production of the one by the other is the underlying or metaphysical connection between them, simply because there is no *underlying* connection. There may be only the connection that we observe.

To assert that this connection may be an ultimate fact which does not stand in need of any metaphysical account is not to prematurely give up the effort to understand the mind-body relation. For there is no good reason to suppose that every state of affairs stands in need of such an account. On the contrary, there is reason to suppose that this is not the case. If it were necessary to account for every state of affairs in terms of something more fundamental, then it would seem that nothing would get accounted for. Rather, there must be some states of affairs so fundamental that they constitute the ultimate facts about our world in terms of which we account for everything else. If there must be such a state of affairs, then it doesn't seem so implausible to suppose that the mind-brain relation is one of them.

If it is a fact that this connection, i.e., this close temporal and constant conjunction, is an ultimate fact in that it cannot be accounted for other than in the sense of describing more completely what other things are associated with it, this would not entail that consciousness would cease to exist with the death of the body. It may be that death results in the dissolution of the connection between consciousness and the brain, but does not destroy both members that were connected. If the connection consists in mere constant conjunction, in merely occurring together regularly, then there would be no reason for thinking that either depends for its existence on the other. By way of contrast, if the connection consisted in the production or creation of consciousness by the brain, then the destruction of the brain would destroy consciousness also. It is the notion of production which implies an existence-dependency relationship, not the concept of a connection consisting merely in two different kinds of things occurring together regularly.

In conclusion, if the connection that we observe involves nothing more than what we observe, then the question as to whether consciousness will continue to exist after the death of the brain is left open. If, on the other hand, this connection that we observe is to be accounted for in terms of something we do not observe, that is, in terms of either selective transmission or production as the mode of connection, then again the question about survival is left open. For then the answer to the question depends upon which of the two is the actual mode of connection, and, as we have seen, there is no basis for preferring the production view over the selective transmission view. In other words, survival of consciousness after brain death is a possibility for either alternative. But, of course, survival may be a possibility without being in fact the case. It may be possible without being actual. To determine whether consciousness and the self actually survive death, we must look at the alleged evidence that some people have survived death and have managed to communicate that fact to the living.

6

A CONCEPTION OF SURVIVING IN ANOTHER WORLD

As we noted earlier, one of the seemingly powerful objections to the belief in a life after death is the argument that we cannot imagine or form any conception of what such a life could be. Since bodily death results in the destruction of the brain, the nervous system, the sense organs, and the rest of the body as well, it would seem that this is not only the end of life, but that any life beyond death is unthinkable. How can we conceive of seeing without eyes, hearing without ears, touching or feeling without a nervous system, thinking or remembering without a brain, and acting upon a world without a physical body? The claim that we shall survive death is not merely false. It is meaningless—completely unintelligible—because we cannot even conceive of a post-mortem existence. Thus we do not even know what we are talking about when we talk about surviving death.

This argument has persuaded many intelligent people to conclude that talk about surviving death doesn't even make sense. It has persuaded them to regard the alleged evidence that some people have survived death as consisting of either false claims or claims which must be reinterpreted as evidence for something other than survival. This is understandable, for it would seem that we cannot have evidence for something which is totally unintelligible. Thus it is apparent how any investigation of the evidence for survival depends upon our being able to arrive at a conception of what survival of death could be. Such a conception is crucial to any view of survival of bodily death.

In this chapter, I shall point out that though the argument that survival is inconceivable may seem to be unassailable, in fact it is not. I shall argue that we *can* conceive of the self continuing to exist and having experiences after bodily death, and of the world it could encounter. However, in doing so I shall be concerned with what we can *conceive* without contradiction to be the case and not, at the moment, with whether or not it is *in fact* the case. In other words, I shall confine my efforts here to a consideration of the *meaning* of the claim that we shall survive, and not with its truth or falsity, or with an evaluation of the alleged evidence that at least some people have survived death.

Some philosophers have argued that the question about survival is self-contradictory and thus absurd because it is a question about whether something is alive at a time when it is no longer alive. This would be a very serious concern if consciousness and the self were not distinguishable from the body. But since they are, the question of survival is rendered clear, at least at this level: Can the conscious self survive the death of the physical body? In other words, the basis for the distinction between consciousness and the body solves this difficulty.

DISEMBODIED PERCEPTION

If we are to conceive of the self surviving the death of the body, we must be able to conceive of the experience that it could have. And this, the skeptic will say, is just the problem. How can we conceive of a disembodied self (a self which death has separated from its body) having experience? It would have no brain, no nervous system, and no sense organs. Part of the solution to this difficulty involves the use of distinctions already made. Since consciousness is distinct from brain activity, we can, without contradiction, ascribe conscious states to a disembodied self. Of course, it may be that consciousness depends for its existence on the brain, in which case as a matter of *fact* it would not continue after the brain dies. But this is not the point at issue. The question is whether we can *conceive* of consciousness occurring independently of the brain, and the answer is that we *can* because consciousness and brain activity are *different* things. In other words, we can conceive of this simply because we can *think* of the one without thinking of the other. They are different things and thus distinguishable in *thought*, however closely connected they may be while the self is embodied.

Since consciousness and brain activity are conceptually distinct, there would seem to be no problem in thinking of various kinds of conscious activities (namely, cognitive activities such as thinking, conceiving, wondering, believing, and doubting) occurring in the absence of a brain. But what, our skeptic may ask, would there be to think about, to conceive? There would be no supply of sensory stimuli to a disembodied self because it would lack sense organs and a nervous system. Thus it could have no sense perception. But without sense perception it would no longer have any means of being aware of a world of material objects. And this would reduce the variety and quality of experience almost to the vanishing point. If we could no longer see or hear or taste or smell, the experiential residue, if any, would be very pale and thin indeed. Moreover, without sense perception it is difficult to see how we could have any emotions or desires. For, in our present state, it seems that all our emotions and desires are either directly or indirectly concerned with objects of sense perception, which includes, of course, our own bodies and those of others.

It appears, then, that there is a problem in conceiving of how a disembodied self could have perceptual experiences and that this problem threatens the very conception of a disembodied self. But this problem disappears when we reflect upon the fact that when we dream we have perceptual-like experience which is independent of the activity of our sense organs. When we dream we seem to see even though our eyes are closed and seem to hear even though there is no sound in the room. Thus since dreams involve perceptual (or, at any rate, perceptual-like) experience which is not generated by our sense organs, they suggest to us how we can conceive of a disembodied self having perceptual experience and thereby apprehending a perceptual world even though it has no sense organs. That is, we can conceive of a disembodied self encountering a perceptual world of the sort that we experience while we dream.

Professor H.H. Price, in a lecture entitled, "Survival and the Idea of Another World,"[1] utilizes the dream experience in this way and thereby provides us with a clearly conceivable and plausible "Next World." This "Next World" or conceivable world of a disembodied self would be of the sort that we encounter when we dream. When we are asleep, stimuli from the sense organs are cut off, or, at any rate, fail to have their usual effects upon the brain. Yet we are sometimes able to have experience in spite of this, for example, when we dream. Though we may decline to say that we perceive when we dream, we must admit that something very much like perception does occur. Since we ordinarily suppose that our image-producing powers generate the dream experience we might prefer to say that we form images rather than perceive while we dream. But, whatever terminology we use, the fact remains that in our dreams we apprehend persons, objects, and events in a manner which is remarkably like perception. These dream entities are more or less similar to those which we perceive normally as a result of the stimuli our sense organs receive from the physical world. There are important differences, of course. The objects that we are aware of in our dreams are not caused by the stimulation of our sense organs, and they often behave in a way which seems very queer to us when we awaken. But the important point is that these dream entities are apprehended in such a vivid, lifelike, perceptual way that they engage our attention, employ our thoughts, and constitute a world of objects of awareness about which we have emotions and desires, at least so long as we dream. In short, while dreaming we regard them just as we regard the objects which we perceive when awake.

The "Next World," then, if there is one, could be a world of mental images, like the world of our dreams. As Price puts it, it could be an "imagy" world. But it would not be imaginary like the Land of Oz, about which we can form images, but which we believe does not exist. Imagining usually means entertaining propositions without believing them. Usually, such propositions are false. Centaurs and unicorns are imaginary in this sense. But there is nothing imaginary about a mental image. It is as real as anything can be. And in this conception it is the substance of what would be the perceptual world of a disembodied self, in that imagining would replace the perceiving which is normally caused by stimulation of the sense organs. Imagining would perform the function which perceiving performs now, namely, the function of providing us with objects which engage our thought and attention and about which we can have emotions and desires. This "imagy" world would be just as real to a disembodied self as the world of sense perception is to us, or as real as the objects of our dreams seem to us to be while we are dreaming. Though we sometimes say that the objects of our dreams are not real (as when someone states, for example, that it was not a real accident that he witnessed, but merely a dream), what we mean is that although they resemble physical objects they are not really physical. For they certainly are real in the sense that they do exist.

But even though we cannot deny that images are real, an image world may nevertheless seem thin and insubstantial compared to our world of physical objects. It may seem that a mere image is to a percept as a shadow is to the object which casts it. Furthermore, an image world would be private like the dream world, whereas the material world is a public one. However, a closer look at the relationship between percepts and images reveals the perceptual world of waking experience to be remarkably similar in some respects to the image world that I have been describing. When we examine the way in which our sense organs and nervous system function in the perceptual process, the whole idea of an image world becomes much more attractive. Let us see how this comes about.

Most people subscribe to a view of perception which philosophers and others have termed "naive realism." This is the view of common sense. According to this view, perception is a process by which we directly apprehend material objects just as they really are in themselves. It is a direct confrontation between observer and object. Our sense organs, when functioning correctly, are like cameras or mirrors, accurately portraying to consciousness the various features of the material world. The grapefruit which we perceive as round, yellow, soft, and smooth really has these features in itself, independently of perception. Of course, the man of common sense has probably not articulated to himself his view in this way. Common sense is not a well-thought-out or highly articulated view. But if caused to reflect on the relation between perception and the physical world, the ordinary person would probably find that he viewed the matter in this way.

Now, presumptuous as it may sound, it is almost a certainty that common sense is mistaken about this. We find that our sense organs do not function like telescopes or mirrors, accurately transmitting or reflecting the features of objects without alteration, but more like transducers or transformers, transforming the stimuli they receive into different energy forms. And the same is true of the nervous system which receives the messages from the senses. Consider what happens in a case of vision— a simple case of, say, seeing a chair. Physicists will tell us that the physical nature of the chair is such that it reflects some of the electromagnetic waves which fall upon it. If these waves (which are invisible, inaudible, and intangible) are of a certain length, they will, when focused by the lens of the eye on the retina, cause chemical reactions in the cells in the retina. These chemical transformations are transduced into electrical form as they travel through the optic nerve to the occipital lobe of the brain. There in the brain a vast electrochemical disturbance occurs as a response to the stimulation by the optic nerve. Nerve impulses, primarily electrical in nature, travel along the axons of neurons, and chemical transformations occur in the synapses between the neurons. And then, as this disturbance occurs, a most wonderful thing happens (although, because of its familiarity, we may not appreciate how remarkable it is): there is an experience of seeing a chair. That is, the percipient sees something of specific color, shape, and size which he calls a chair.

Of course, visual perception is much more detailed and complex than the rather simple account that I have presented. But even this simplified account reveals numer-

ous and profound transformations taking place in the
process of visual perception. Energy is being transformed from one form to another as the message travels
from eye to brain. But by far the most amazing part of
the process is the visual experience of seeing a chair
which occurs in conjunction with the electrochemical
disturbance in the brain. Let us call what is seen a visual
percept. It has color, shape, and size; and common sense
calls it a chair. But note that, if this account of the process of visual perception is essentially correct, the visual
percept cannot be identified with the physical object out
there in the external world reflecting the electromagnetic
waves. There is nothing in this account to suggest that
they are even very similar. The visual percept, for example, has color. But there is no reason to think that the
physical object which causes this percept to arise in one's
experience has any color. The electromagnetic waves
which it reflects have no color. Physicists tell us that they
are invisible. Indeed, they are totally insensible in themselves. But those with the right length (viz., those between .0007 and .0004 of a millimeter) *cause* us to see
color, even though they are not themselves colored.
Moreover, according to atomic theory, the physical object is composed of a vast concatenation of atoms, each
of which is composed of protons, electrons, neutrons,
and other sub-atomic particles. But the atoms are not
colored, nor are the sub-atomic particles. It does not even
make sense to say that they are.

A similar account can be given in the case of all the
other senses. An external stimulus reaches the sense organ and is transformed by it. As a consequence of this,
a message in primarily electrical form travels along the
nerve connecting the sense organ to the brain. A vast
electrochemical disturbance occurs in the portions of the
brain to which the nerve connects, and, along with this
disturbance, the appropriate sense experience takes place.

This view of perception which, incidentally, is based

upon what the natural sciences have discovered about the nature and function of the sense organs and nervous system, has been called a causal theory of perception. For it holds that the relation between the physical object and what is perceived (i.e., the percept) is a causal one. The physical object causes the percept but is not identical with it. They cannot be identical, for they not only have different features but there is a time lag between them. The percept occurs somewhat later than the stimulus provided by the physical object; for it takes time for the stimulus to travel from the physical object to the perceiver's body (when they are not in contact) and more time to travel through the sense organ and nervous system of the perceiver. Though this time lag is so small that it has no practical importance in most cases and thus normally goes unnoticed, its existence is very apparent in the case of the perception of distant objects such as stars. When I perceive a star which is, say, 40,000 light years away, what I see is simultaneous with my seeing it. But the physical object which emitted the light may no longer be in existence at that time. What I see, therefore, cannot be the physical object itself, but rather an effect of it. Thus cases of considerable time lag also make it obvious that percepts and physical objects must be distinguished.

The causal theory of perception is what philosophers call a representational view of perception. According to the representational view, the perceiver is never in direct contact with the physical object. What is perceived is always merely a representation of the physical object, and never the object itself. This is a very plausible view that easily explains phenomena such as sensory illusions and sensory deficits (such as color blindness) which remain puzzling in other views. Long before we knew much about the way our sense organs and nervous system function, philosophers were arguing for representationalism because they observed that what we perceive varies with the conditions under which we perceive it. For example, snow looks pink when perceived through rose-colored glasses, a straight stick appears bent when partially submerged in water, and objects appear somewhat yellow colored when one has jaundice. But the physical objects themselves do not vary with these conditions. They have nothing to do with the objects as such. The natures of the physical objects around me certainly do not change as I become infected with jaundice. But if what we perceive varies while the physical object remains unchanged, then what we perceive cannot be the physical object itself, but, at best, some representation of it.

Now, if what we perceive (viz., percepts) must be distinguished from the objects in the physical world, the differences between percepts and images diminish and seem less important. There is less inclination to regard images as insubstantial when compared with percepts if neither is to be construed as a part of the physical world. Moreover, if representationalism is correct, percepts would be private just as images are. If what I see when I look at a chair is a percept conjoined with my brain response, it would seem that my percept is distinct from yours just as our brains are distinct. If you and I are looking at the same chair from the same distance and perspective, then what I see would be exactly similar to what you see. But, it would seem, they cannot be one and the same percept. One might even wonder if they could ever be even exactly similar, since it would seem to be extremely unlikely that two people would have exactly similar sense organs, exactly similar brains and nervous systems, and would be able to attain exactly similar perspectives.

A moment's reflection will, I think, convince us that we must have been, at some level, regarding percepts as private even if we were not aware of the considerations just advanced. Consider the case of a person who is partially color blind and cannot distinguish red from green. It is obvious that we cannot directly inspect his experience and visually observe how what we call red and green appear to him. We have to *infer* this blindness by giving him a test or by observing in some other way his behavior in the presence of those colors. And, of course, the same is true with respect to the other senses. We cannot directly apprehend the sensory experience of another just as we cannot feel his pain.

Now, if percepts and images are alike in that both are private and neither can be identified with any physical things in the external world, then a Next World of dream-like images could be just like the present world of waking experience insofar as its sensory aspects are concerned. That is to say, in dreams—especially vivid ones—we see colors, hear pitches and tones, and sometimes smell, taste, and feel the textures and temperatures of objects in the dream just as clearly and indubitably as when awake. If we call this the sensory content, then it is apparent that the sensory content of dreams (and that of the Next World of images, if there is one) is just like that of waking experience. Furthermore, just as in waking experience, this sensory content is organized in such a way as to form objects—the objects which we encounter in our dreams. Of course, these objects often behave in strange ways but this is not surprising since the cause of dream experience is quite different from that of waking experience.

What I am suggesting, then, is that if the Next World is conceived as an image world like that of our dreams, it could be expected to be similar to the world we encounter when awake with respect to *what* we experience (i.e., the sensory data organized so as to form objects) though not with respect to *how* that experience comes about. The difference would consist not primarily in the content but in the *cause* of experience. But because the causes differ we might expect that the laws governing the behavior of objects in the Next World would be quite different from the natural law of this world. However, in spite of these considerations, it may seem that there is one very important respect in which the world of a disembodied subject of experience would differ from our world and that this difference threatens the very conceivability of such a world. Since a disembodied self would, of course, have no physical body, his sensory experience would have to be quite different from any we have had. But this is really not a serious problem. Though a disembodied subject could not have a physical body, he could nevertheless experience himself as having a body—a body which could appear so much like his former physical body that he mistakenly believes it to be physical.

To see how this is possible, a comparison of this Next World with the dream world may again be helpful. When one dreams he frequently finds himself to be embodied in the dream world. Many of one's dreams are such that they involve the activities of an apparently embodied person whom one takes to be oneself as long as one dreams. I have, for example, occasionally dreamed that I was looking at myself in a mirror. In the dreams, I had no doubt that I was the being whose reflection I saw in the mirror. I carefully noted my facial features and clearly remembered them upon awakening. Whatever is the source of the imagery of my dreams apparently has the capacity to bring about images of a human body and to impart the feeling that that body is mine. It is, of course, just an image body, but it serves as a perfectly good body for the dream experience. I regard it as mine, I act on the dream environment by means of it, and it constitutes the center of the perceptual world of my dream.

Now, it is certainly conceivable that a disembodied subject could have a set of relatively persistent images which he regarded as his own body and which would constitute the constant center of his perceptual world. It would be a body of the sort that we sometimes dream that we have. This is understandable, for when embodied, one would have had various perceptual experiences of his body—mainly visual and tactual, but also bodily feelings. After death and disembodiment he is no longer capable of having experiences of a physical body, but it is certainly conceivable that he would retain memory images of them. And it is conceivable that under certain conditions memory images would have the forcefulness, the vividness, the striking, attention-arresting quality of the perceptual experiences of which they are the images.

Note that memory images are (what we might call) paler, fainter, weaker, less vivid, less vivacious than the perceptual experiences of which they are the images. This difference is hard to describe but should be obvious to anyone. Perceptual experiences are undeniably different in nature from memory images of them. Each of us knows from his own case what this difference is and has no difficulty using this knowledge to distinguish perception and memory. But perceptual experiences do not differ in a similar way from the perceptual-like experiences of our dreams. Indeed, dream imagery is much more like percepts than like memory imagery. Dream imagery, or a great deal of it at any rate, has that vivid, striking quality of percepts. Dreaming that you are, for example, looking at your automobile is much more like actually seeing it than it is like the memory image of it that you have when you are remembering what it looks like. Now let us see how this relates to the brain.

We have already examined the view that the brain functions as a selective transmitter or inhibitor of consciousness and found it to be a plausible one. Now suppose that this view is true, or at least partially true, and that one of the functions of the brain is to inhibit or to subdue the forcefulness and vivacity of memory images. Such suppression would certainly have survival value. We would frequently be in great trouble if we were susceptible to confusion about whether we were actually seeing something or merely remembering something we have seen. If we were susceptible to a confusion which would sometimes lead us to conclude that we are merely remembering standing on the track and observing the oncoming train when in fact we are currently perceiving this, we would probably not survive very long. Suppose further that during sleep this inhibitory function is relaxed, allowing memory to manifest itself in the dream experience, and that at death when biological needs no longer exist, it ceases altogether. With the disappearance of the inhibitor, memory images would attain the forcefulness and vivacity of dream imagery and ordinary sense perception. In addition, it may be that when memory is no longer inhibited either in forcefulness or extent, the disembodied self would have memory images of virtually everything that happened to him while embodied, in which case his experience after disembodiment would be very rich indeed.

Now, if the images that a disembodied subject has of his body are based upon memories of his experiences when embodied, his image body would appear to him to be very much like the physical body he formerly had. And if this image body had the forcefulness and vivacity of dream images (or percepts)—as we might expect when memory images are no longer suppressed—and if it formed the persistent center of his perceptual world (remaining relatively constant while other images change), it would have both the appearance and the function of the physical body he once had. Thus the world that he finds himself in may seem to him to be so much like this one that it may take some time for him to realize that he is no longer embodied. Indeed, he may eventually arrive at the true conclusion not because his body or the objects around him look or feel different from that to which he is accustomed, but because he discovers that these image bodies are subject to peculiar causal laws. For example, he may find that (what to him are) the features of his world (or to us are his images) alter in accordance with his wishes. More specifically, he may find that a wish to travel to (what to him is) a certain place is immediately followed by clusters of vivid and detailed images which in his world would be that place. He would come to realize that traveling or transferring his body from place to place is a very different process from what it used to be, and thus he may be led to conclude that he now has a different sort of body which has the appearance of his former body but different causal properties. And upon closer examination of the objects composing his world, he may discover that although they have the usual sensory properties such as color, weight, shape, and size, they too have strange causal properties. He may find his wish for a certain object followed, as in our daydreams, by the images which now constitute that object. In other words, he may discover that he can change his environment, or parts of it, in a manner similar to the way we change our imagined environment when we daydream. Such observations would provide him with a basis for concluding that he is now in a different world.

There should be no problem in conceiving of a wish-fulfillment world or in understanding why the world of this disembodied being might be just such a world. Since our dreams, as well as our daydreams and our imaginings, are influenced if not determined by our desires, a wish-fulfillment world is the very world we ought to expect on the assumption that the world in question is composed of the stuff of dreams and daydreams. But it is important to notice that not all parts of a wish-fulfillment world need be under conscious control. This is important because if all events in such a world must be under conscious control, the world of our disembodied being would be vastly different from our own—so different that we may have trouble understanding what it would be like. But any problem that might threaten to arise here can be avoided by supposing that the disembodied being has wishes of a deep-seated nature which are unconscious or unacknowledged. Surely the notion of unconscious desires is no longer strange. But if it should seem problematic, one can do without it by appealing to the fact that some desires are not subject to conscious control, or to the fact that though our dreams are influenced by our desires, we have little if any ability to determine the content of our dreams. In other words, there are various ways of supporting the view that a being in a wish-fulfillment world could be presented with *involuntary* images. And if he is presented with involuntary as well as voluntary images, his world could appear to him to be very much like our world (i.e., the world he inhabited when he was embodied). For what we interpret as a distinction between voluntary and involuntary images could appear to him as a distinction between what he does to his environment and what his environment does to him. That is, he could regard the images under voluntary control as his actions in and upon his environment, and the involuntary images as events that happen to him in that environment.

It is worth noting that this distinction between voluntary and involuntary images gives more precision to the concept of the image body of a disembodied self. His body would consist of clusters of involuntary images which form the center of his image world and which remain relatively constant while other images change. In being involuntary, they would be like the percepts we have of our physical bodies.

LOCATION OF DISEMBODIED SUBJECTS

Since image bodies, like physical bodies, have shape, size, and color, and are therefore extended in space, it is obvious that the image body world is a spatial one. But if it is, we might wonder *where* it is. And here a problem seems to arise. This world, if it exists, must be somewhere, and yet there seems to be no room for it in the physical universe. It is surely not up in the sky, or on some other planet, or even in another galaxy. The problem is not to be solved by looking for this world in physical space. But the solution is apparent when we realize that such a world can be a spatial one without being in (or bearing any spatial relationship to) physical space. To see how this can be the case, let us again consider the dream experience. It is obvious that dream images have spatial features. Visual images have shape, size, and color, and are thus extended in space. Moreover, they bear spatial relations to each other. Suppose that I dream of a deer emerging from a forest with a wolf in pursuit. The deer image is certainly spatially related to the wolf image and both bear spatial relationships to the forest. But they are not spatially related to anything in the physical world. If you were to ask me where this episode took place—in Minnesota? in Canada? or where?—I would be unable to answer other than to reply that the question is absurd. I am unable to answer not because I lack the necessary information, but because the question is meaningless. Such things cannot be located in physical space. They are in space, and each of them is somewhere in relation to other images that I have. But they are in a space which bears no spatial relationship to physical space.

Thus, the world of a disembodied self should be regarded in the same way. For, as we have been conceiving it, it is a dream-like world of images. Like the dream world, it is a spatial world which has a space of its own and which bears no spatial relationship to physical space. Though we cannot find it in the physical world and ought not look for it there, this fact surely does not imply that it cannot exist as a spatial world. There is certainly no *a priori* reason why all spatial entities must be in the physical space. It follows from these considerations that passing from this world to the next should not be regarded as some sort of movement in space but as a change in consciousness analogous to that which we experience when we awaken from a dream.

DISEMBODIED COMMUNICATION

It may be argued that although this conception of the world of a disembodied subject is intelligible it is not very attractive in that it is a private mind-dependent world in which the solitary subject, alone with his images, is cut off from all communications and social relations with other selves. Though one could remember, perhaps even vividly and totally, communications and relations with others when embodied, it would seem that one would be completely cut off from any further communication with others. And if this were the case, one might wonder how long the personality of a disembodied self would remain intact.

The first point to note about this argument is its suggestion that since the image world is a private, mind-dependent world whereas this world is public and mind-independent, it is less real or less valuable as a world because of that. As we have seen, however, if the representational view of perception is correct (and there is good reason for thinking that it is), the sensory content of this world is private and mind-dependent also. The difference in regard to the question of privacy consists in the fact that most of the sensory content of this world has a public, mind-independent *cause* (consisting in material objects and other people), whereas this is not true of the sensory content of the image world. But when one realizes that the sensory content in both worlds is private, there should be little inclination to regard the image world as some sort of deception or sham world, less real than this one.

The problem about communication with others is more serious. In this world, communication with others is possible via the effects we have on each other's sense organs. By speaking and thereby setting up a series of vibrations in the air which affect your ears, I can induce in you auditory sensations which you interpret as expressing my thoughts, feelings, and wishes. By gesturing, writing, and using facial expressions, I can induce visual sensations in you which you interpret in the same way. But these methods of communication depend upon the existence of air, electromagnetic waves, physical sense organs, nerves, and brains, and these material things would not exist in the image world. Though a disembodied subject may experience himself as having sense organs, they could be no more physical than the sense organs of the bodies we sometimes dream that we have. Thus our normal methods of communication would not work in such a world.

It is conceivable, however, that a disembodied subject would be able to communicate with other disembodied beings in a more direct way which does not depend upon the mediation and proper functioning of sense organs, nerves, and brain. He may find that he can directly affect the consciousness of another in a manner which, when it occurs in this world, is called mental telepathy. The evidence that at least some people can at times exercise telepathic powers is impressive and becoming stronger. Mental telepathy is one of the best, if not the best, attested form of extrasensory perception. It would seem, however, that the sort of mental telepathy by which one may in this world be able to affect the thoughts of another would not by itself be sufficient for communication. For this sort of telepathy would not allow one to identify the being who was telepathically affecting his thought, or to know (or even, perhaps, surmise) that the anomaly in the pattern of his thought was due to the efforts of another. But there is another sort of telepathy which could, at least when coupled with other forms of telepathy, make communication possible, namely the sort of telepathy which

in this world produces telepathic apparitions. Suppose
that the image body of our disembodied being very
closely resembles his former physical body. Suppose further that he is able to cause in the experience of other
disembodied beings a telepathic apparition which very
closely resembles his image body (and, of course, his
former physical body as well), and that they, in turn,
could cause in his experience telepathic apparitions resembling their former physical bodies. Now, telepathic
apparitions are not, even in this world, entirely visual;
sometimes apparitional sounds are heard to issue from
the visual portion of the apparition. So let us suppose
that by means of the telepathic apparition of his image
body, a disembodied being induces in other such beings
auditory sensations of the sentences which express the
thoughts he wishes to communicate (without, of course,
the mediation of sound waves). As he does this, he also
induces similar auditory sensations in himself such that
he is able to "hear himself talk," much as he could when
he was embodied. And if he, as well as other disembodied beings, could engage in such activities, they could
have an experience of communicating with each other
which is very similar to that which we have now—so
similar, it may temporarily prevent them from realizing
that they are disembodied.

Perhaps these speculations about the telepathic powers
of a disembodied self seem fantastic. But they are conceivable. And they may not be as fantastic as they seem.
There is fairly good evidence that extrasensory perception (of which mental telepathy is a species) sometimes
occurs in this world. Parapsychologists and psychical researchers (e.g., J.B. Rhine) cite numerous spontaneous
cases as well as experimental results which strongly suggest that some people are sometimes able to acquire information about the thoughts of others and about the
world other than by way of their senses (i.e., telepathically and clairvoyantly) and to affect the material world

without using the body to do it (i.e., psychokinetically). In other words, these people have gone a long way toward establishing the existence of what J.B. Rhine has called a ''psi'' capacity. And it may be that psi is an integral part of this world. It certainly has such a status in an intriguing theory proposed by Thouless and Wiesner.[2] They suggest that in normal sense perception the self finds out what is going on in the sensory part of its nervous system by means of psi. And in normal volition it affects its nervous system by means of psi. The famous psychical researcher F.W.H. Myers expresses the same idea when, in an effort to explain hypnotic phenomena in terms of psi, he writes, ''perhaps when I *attend* to a thing, or *will* a thing, I am directing upon my own nervous system actually that same force which, when I direct it on another man's nervous system, is the 'vital influence' of mesmerists, or the 'telepathic impact' of which Mr. Gurney and I have said so much.''[3] In other words what happens in extrasensory perception is of essentially the same nature as what happens in our normal cognitive processes, and what happens in psychokinesis is of essentially the same nature as that which happens in our normal voluntary behavior. The difference is that in the former cases the self interacts directly with the external world whereas in the latter, normal situations, the self interacts directly with the brain and only indirectly with everything else in the external world.

In this view, when the self is affected by its nervous system or body, which, to be non-specific, we may call its ''soma,'' the result is ordinary perception. On the other hand, when the self is directly affected by an external object (other than its soma), the result is clairvoyant perception. When the self acts upon its soma, the result is an ordinary act of will. And when the self acts directly upon an external object (other than its soma) the result is what we call psychokinesis. One might say that ordinary perception is just endo-somatic clairvoyance and clairvoyance is merely exo-somatic perception. Similarly, ordinary volition turns out to be just endo-somatic psychokinesis and psychokinesis is merely exo-somatic volition.

A consequence of this view is that telepathy, clairvoyance, psychokinesis, and other forms of psi should not be regarded as paranormal (i.e., in direct conflict with the fundamental presuppositions of common sense and its scientific extensions). Instead, they should be viewed as instances of processes which in themselves are normal and even familiar, but as occurring in a manner which is not familiar. As Thouless and Wiesner put it,

> They may be no more ''paranormal'' than the facts following from Einstein's theory of relativity. Physicists do not regard the Newtonian laws of motion as ''normal'' and those motion and gravitational effects which follow the principles of relativity as paranormal; they regard the Newtonian principles as a special case of a more general set of principles which includes also the relativity phenomenon. This special case happens to be more familiar than the exceptions to it because most observable phenomena of movement occur within the limits of velocity for which Newtonian principles are approximately true. If we had been born in a universe in which all velocities of bodies were near that of light, then the Einstein laws would have been the familiar ones.[4]

Similarly, the familiar way in which we learn about and act upon the world, namely, by way of our nervous systems and bodies, may be just a special case of a wider phenomenon which includes every case of the self interacting with its world. Our ordinary interaction with this world is limited to that very small portion of it which consists in the nervous system of our body. But we might have found ourselves in a world with which we could interact other than in this limited way. In such a world the various forms of psi would be as familiar as they are now uncommon.

Thus, if psi is as widespread and pervasive as the Thouless-Wiesner theory indicates, the claim that disembodied subjects could employ it in their communication with one another becomes much more plausible. Though what is widespread in their view is endo-somatic psi, one can conceivably explain the apparent rarity of exo-somatic psi along lines already suggested. If the brain functions as an awareness inhibitor, restricting attention to what is more or less of immediate practical concern to the physical organism in its struggle for survival, then any capacity which is not particularly conducive to success in that struggle would tend to be suppressed. And if our psi capacity is now being suppressed because of the priority of bodily needs, then we might expect it to be released in the absence of a body.

DISEMBODIED IDENTITY

The task of presenting a detailed conception of a Next World in which a disembodied subject could have a rich variety of experiences is now almost complete. There remains one final matter which, though it may seem rather abstruse, must be taken into account because it has been considered by some very respectable philosophers to be a serious objection to the possibility of an afterlife as disembodied existence in another realm. There are philosophers who doubt that we can conceive of a person having a continuous history, that is, of remaining one and the same person throughout time in the absence of bodily continuity. Although we change in various ways (in shape, size, physical appearance, thoughts, beliefs, attitudes, etc.), we regard ourselves as remaining one and the same person throughout our lifetimes. But we are to do this, such philosophers would contend, only because our bodies are continuously in existence during this time. In other words, our personal identity depends upon the continuous existence of our bodies. Thus, they would argue, the disembodied existence of a person after death is unintelligible because, in the absence of the body, no account can be given of how a disembodied subject can be identified with anyone who was embodied or how he can remain one and the same person through time. Terence Penelhum, for example, claims that "the doctrine of disembodied survival founders because no intelligible account seems possible in it of the persistence of a disembodied person through time."[5]

Now, it is true that we normally identify people other than ourselves by means of their bodies. Moreover, we function through our bodies and exist in such close relationship with them that our thoughts of ourselves as continuous beings are, in practice, closely tied up with the continuity of our bodies. In normal situations the presence of the same body is a perfectly good guarantee of the presence of the same person. But this fact in itself does not tell us what the identity of a person consists in. It shows merely that bodily continuity can normally be regarded as a guarantee of personal identity. Thus the former may be merely a good indicator of the latter, but not an essential constituent.

As we attempt to determine that in which personal identity consists, we must distinguish two different ways in which we identify things. We normally identify things by locating or describing them. Unless I can indicate in some way the thing I am referring to, I will not be able to communicate with someone else. Thus I must either locate (perhaps by pointing) the thing to which I am referring or else provide some sort of description of it. But there is an element of arbitrariness in what we take to be an individual thing because we can draw the boundaries of things in a number of different ways depending upon a combination of what we find in the world in conjunction with our interests and purposes. A chair, for example, may be regarded as an individual thing. But it is composed of legs, seat, and back which in turn are composed of parts which can be further divided into parts without end. If one is thinking of a house complete with furniture, then the chair is a part of that larger unit. If one is thinking of furniture, the unit is the chair. But if one of the legs is damaged, then the unit is the leg or perhaps some part of it such as a cracked bracket or missing screw. Thus the individual things that we acknowledge depend partly upon what we find in the world and partly upon our purposes.

This element of arbitrariness can be a source of difficulty for us when we try to decide whether or not something has remained one and the same thing over a period of time. Consider the case of a much-used automobile which has been repaired so many times that none of the original parts remain. Is it the same automobile or not? It seems that we could answer either way. The nature of the case does not dictate one answer to the exclusion of the other. That is, an examination of the nature of an automobile doesn't provide an answer. Rather, the answer seems to be, at least in part, a verbal matter—a matter of convention.

When we apply this method of identification to persons, we ascribe to them a history and various characteristics. A certain person was born on a particular day, has a name, is married, has three children, went to college, is employed as an insurance salesman, likes to do crossword puzzles, and is an enthusiastic hockey fan. We think that the more we know of such matters, the better we know the person. And we can identify him by giving a description involving these characteristics. We can identify ourselves in the same manner, building a conception of ourselves based upon what we have done and what has happened to us. We can give a description of ourselves just as we can of others.

We are so familiar with this manner of identification that we may fail to notice that there is one case where we can identify without giving a description—the case where I identify myself *to* myself. I know what it is to be myself in a manner that does not involve knowledge of my personal history or characteristics. However much knowledge I have of these things, it is not knowledge of what it is for this history or these characteristics to be mine. In this most fundamental sense of identity, I would know myself to be the self that I am even if these things were different so that I would have to give a different description of myself. H.D. Lewis gives a clear statement of this point:

> There is a radically different sense in which I know myself to be this I that I am whatever the particular story which I (or someone else) tells about me. Irrespective of what I feel or think, I am the being I am, and would be if the story were different. This is what I call the basic sense of identity in which everyone knows who he is however little he may say about it or reflect upon it.[6]

It is important to note that this fundamental knowledge of who I am is not at all a matter of convention. I am myself—the unique irreducible being that I find myself to be. I could not be any other. This is not a verbal matter. I cannot even conceive of failing to know myself as the being that I am. Of course, I can conceive of losing my memory, in which case I could not give a description of my history or characteristics and thus could not identify myself in the first-mentioned sense. But even in such a predicament, I would still be aware that this is happening to me and would still know myself as the being that I find myself to be.

Now, a disembodied self would identify himself in this fundamental sense. To be a self he must have experiences, and in having experience he would know himself as the being he finds himself to be. He would know himself in the fundamental way in which we know ourselves now. But personal identity, at least in this sense, does not depend upon bodily continuity. One has it in the dream, the out-of-the-body experience, and all other imaginable experiences. And this is the fundamental kind since it is present when the other is present and remains even when the other has disappeared. However, more than this sense of self is required if a disembodied subject is to be able to identify himself with a person who was embodied, and to experience himself as remaining one and the same self with the passage of time. For this requires memory. He must be able to remember experiences that he had while embodied to accomplish the former task and to remember experiences that he had after disembodiment to accomplish the latter.

But it is at this point, the critic will contend, that the notion of disembodied existence breaks down. He will argue that memory cannot be used as a basis for the personal identity of a disembodied self because it is dependent upon bodily continuity. The argument, as advanced by critics such as S. Shoemaker[7] and T. Penelhum, involves a distinction between two senses of the word "remember"—a strong and a weak sense. Sometimes we actually remember and at other times we merely seem to remember. Let us call the strong sense remembering$_1$, and the weak sense, remembering$_2$. Then one can express this distinction by saying that if a subject remembers$_1$ having an experience, then he really did have it; whereas if he remembers$_2$ having an experience, then he may not have had it. In other words, to say that a subject remembers$_2$ is to say no more than that he claims to remember$_1$. And, of course, his claim may be false.

Penelhum uses this distinction in an attempt to show that no account of disembodied identity can be given. Penelhum points out that any account of disembodied identity must involve remembering in the strong sense.

But then he says, "This requires that we should be able to distinguish between those occasions when what someone thinks he remembers actually happened to him, and those occasions when they did not. This we cannot do in terms of his recollections themselves. There has to be some independent way of determining that the person who did or experienced what Smith believes he remembers doing or experiencing was, or was not, Smith himself. And this, it seems, has to be his physical presence at the occasion in question."[8] He thinks that "this refutation is in essence correct,"[9] and sufficient to show that there can be no intelligible concept of disembodied existence. But his "refutation" is open to a number of criticisms which appear to demolish it. To begin with, why is it essential that we should be "able to distinguish" between occasions when the disembodied subject actually remembers and occasions when he only seems to remember? Surely there would nevertheless *be* a difference between these two kinds of occasions, even if we (or the subject himself, for that matter) were unable to determine which was which. To maintain otherwise would be to subscribe to the view that if there were no way of telling whether or not two events differ, then there would *be* no difference between them. But this inference from what is or can be *known* to what *is* or *can be* is obviously fallacious.

Furthermore, at least one problem which seems to concern Penelhum disappears when one looks at the matter from the first-person perspective. When I wonder whether I am remembering₁, I am certainly not wondering whether the experience I think I remember belongs to me or someone else. Rather, my concern is with the entirely different matter of whether the experience did in fact occur. For it is clear from the first-person perspective that I could not even seem to remember the experience of someone else.

Of course, in order to conceive of disembodied identity

one must be able to conceive of the distinction between remembering$_1$ and remembering$_2$ in the case of a disembodied subject. But such a conception should not be confused with a way of determining (or telling) whether an act of remembering which occurs under strange circumstances is a remembering$_1$ or a remembering$_2$. Since by reference to physical phenomena we can often *tell* (i.e., verify) whether or not an act of remembering is a remembering$_1$, there is no reason to suppose that we could not even *conceive* of an act as a remembering$_1$ merely because it occurs under circumstances which prevent us from telling whether it is a remembering$_1$ or a remembering$_2$.

But perhaps the attribution of this confusion to Penelhum would be a rather uncharitable interpretation. So let us suppose that what he means to suggest by the phrases "able to distinguish" and "way of determining" is that we must be able to conceive of a disembodied subject remembering in the strong sense, and not, as his words suggest, that unless we could tell, in regard to some particular act of remembering, whether it was a remembering$_1$ or a remembering$_2$, and could tell without reference to any physical characteristics whatever, we could not conceive of a disembodied identity. Surely a conception of a disembodied subject remembering in the strong sense would be sufficient and is thus all that Penelhum is justified in requiring. But if the presence of this concept is all that he is requiring, his "refutation" utterly fails. For there is no problem conceiving of a disembodied subject remembering something which actually happened to him.[10]

We might also question Penelhum's assumption that memory claims require to be checked or verified. We make some memory claims with great confidence. I clearly remember laying a book on the table a short time ago, and my confidence that I actually did this seems to be justified when I take careful note of what we find

memory to be. Somehow I am able to recall the event
with certainty though without any independent confir-
mation of its occurrence. As I remember laying the book
on the table, I seem to possess a knowledge of the past
that is direct and immediate. What I remember must be
distinguished from the memory image that I now have of
laying the book on the table; for the memory image is in
the present, whereas what I remember is part of the past
and thus not in existence anymore. Moreover, my memory image is often inaccurate and known to be so. But I
could not know it to be inaccurate unless I were able to
some extent to compare it with the object or event that
I am remembering. And I could not do this unless what
I am remembering were accessible to me independently
of my memory image of it.

Once we realize that memory provides an immediate
knowledge of the past which must not be confused with
the memory images which often help us remember, we
are in a better position to appreciate that in some fashion,
without being infallible, it provides its own guarantee.
Certainly we are fortunate to the extent that it does this;
for, as Don Locke writes as he concludes his interesting
little book on memory, "memory has to be accepted as
reliable, because without it there would be no knowledge
at all, in particular no knowledge of the past. One cannot
question the possibility of memory-knowledge without
shaking the entire structure of human knowledge to its
foundations."[11] Perhaps Penelhum and Shoemaker would
find themselves in basic agreement with this, for they
admit that it is a necessary truth that memory claims are
usually true.

Now, if memory must be regarded as providing us with
direct knowledge of the past and thereby, in some sense,
guaranteeing itself, it would be very implausible to suppose that the *checking* of memory claims is so essential
that when this cannot be done a person (e.g., a disem-

bodied self) cannot even conceive of remembering something that actually happened to him. Thus there would
seem to be no reason why memory could not be used to
establish the personal identity of a disembodied self, i.e.,
no reason to suppose that it could not serve as the basis
upon which such a being could establish that he had remained one and the same self with the passage of time.
Indeed, it would establish personal identity in the most
complete manner. For when memory provides me with
direct knowledge of the past, I remember it in its fullness
in that I remember not only what happened but also my
own unique awareness of myself at the time. I remember
myself as the being I now find myself to be, and this
enables me to establish my identity through time in the
most complete manner possible; for it includes the distinctive awareness that I have of myself at any time, now
and in the past. It is the basis of my knowledge that I
have remained one and the same being during the interval between the present and the event that I remember.
And it can be used with equal effectiveness in establishing the identity of a disembodied self; for, as we have
seen, there is no reason to think that it is dependent upon
bodily continuity.[12]

But even if we suppose for the sake of the argument
that memory is dependent upon bodily continuity, it is
not obvious that this would render unintelligible the notion of disembodied existence which I have been describing. For, as we have seen, the world of the disembodied
subject does not appear to be very different from our
own, at least in the respects which bear upon personal
identity. The disembodied subject does not have a physical body, but he has an image body which would seem
to have whatever relevance to his identity through time
as our bodies have to ours. It persists relatively unchanged through considerable lengths of time and constitutes the constant center of his image world. Indeed,
if it changed at all, it might change much more gradually

than does ours. Some may be inclined to say that personal identity would not be possible without the continuance of a background of bodily feeling. But whatever function such feelings may serve could be served by the images of them which a disembodied being could have. And though an image body is mind-dependent, we can conceive of another person having a perceptual experience of it if we allow for the possibility of communication via telepathic apparitions. It would be similar to our present perceptual experience of our physical bodies if the representative theory of perception is correct. For, on that theory, the perceptions that we have when we see and feel our bodies are also mind-dependent, even though the physical body itself is not. Image and physical bodies differ with respect to the way in which the perceptions of them are caused, but not in the way they would be perceived by the subject.

It is apparent, then, that the attempt to show that disembodied existence is impossible by linking memory to bodily continuity does not succeed. This should not be surprising. If I am correct in contending that consciousness is radically different from anything physical, and that the self is essentially a conscious being, then it would be strange indeed to find that self-identity is necessarily tied to the continuity of the physical body. Indeed, our nature is such that even if we should lose our memory, and thereby lose that by which we are supposed to be linked with bodily continuity, it would seem that personal identity would remain intact. Although we could then have no *knowledge* of a past experience or of ourselves as having had it, this would not prevent our *having been* the subject of it. We know that the fact that I have forgotten most of my experiences does not prevent me from having been the subject of them. Likewise, a total memory failure would not affect the fact that I would have known myself, in the forgotten experience, as the being that I now know myself to be.[13]

It is important to note that this account of the personal identity of a disembodied subject also provides a solution to a related problem that one may have been wondering about, namely, the problem of determining what it is in virtue of which one such subject *differs* from every other. This is the problem of individuating disembodied subjects—of specifying the basis for distinguishing each subject from every other. One must be able to solve this problem if one is to be able to conceive of a disembodied individual (or disembodied person). It is obvious that one cannot distinguish between two disembodied persons by noting that they are in different (physical) places as one can in the case of the bodies of two embodied persons. But the solution has already been suggested; for whatever helps to account for an individual's being identical with itself through time helps to account for its not being identical with any other individual. The fundamental difference between myself and another is revealed in that very special manner in which I know what it is to be myself in the very fact of being myself and in having the experiences that I have. As I have suggested earlier, when I consider the difference between myself and another from the perspective of my own inner experience, there is absolutely no problem in distinguishing myself from another. From this perspective the difference is incontestable, absolute, and irreducible. I am the being that I know in the process of being myself in my experience, and clearly could be no other. This individuating self-knowledge is so basic that it cannot be described in terms of something more fundamental than itself. And it is knowledge which we have every reason to believe a disembodied individual could have.

However, this fundamental way in which disembodied subjects could be individuated is not the only possible one. For each disembodied subject differs from every other in that he has a different ordered set of experiences—he differs from every other either in the content of his experience or in the order of his experiences or in both these respects. Among other things, they would differ in having different memories of an embodied life. For each is temporally continuous with an embodied subject and each embodied subject must differ from every other either in experience content, or in the order of his experiences, or both. This is because the perceptual experiences of an embodied subject are conditioned by the spatial location of his (physical) body, and no two bodies can be in the same (physical) place at the same time. Thus if a subject is regarded as a single entity including both embodied and disembodied phases, there would be no difficulty in understanding how each differs from every other. Nor is there any difficulty in regarding a subject in this way; for if dream or hallucinatory-type images continue after death, there is no more reason for thinking that personal identity must be broken by death and disembodiment than there is reason for thinking that one's personal identity is broken when one dreams.

The task of presenting a detailed conception of a disembodied subject and of a world in which he could have a rich variety of experiences is now complete. The task was to present a conception which is intelligible, that is, a conception which is understandable because it is internally consistent throughout. Solutions were provided for the problems of identity, of individuation, of spatial location, and of disembodied "perception." And in the process of providing them, some main arguments which have been regarded as showing that this conception is unintelligible were found to be invalid. It was also shown that there is no problem in conceiving of a disembodied being having the various kinds of experiences which justify our regarding this being as a disembodied *self* or *person*. Indeed, it was seen that the experience of such a being could be as rich as our own, and his world could seem much like ours. The conception of this being was described in considerable detail in an effort to uncover any contradictions that might be concealed in it (or, more accurately, concealed in the statements in which it is expressed). And no contradictions were found. Yet there is every reason to think that if there were any we would have found them; for this conception, though rather complex, is not so difficult for us to comprehend because it is of a being much like ourselves in many respects. Indeed, because this conception is of a being much like ourselves, there is hardly any more reason to suspect that it is unintelligible in any way than there is reason to suspect this about our conception of our own selves. Thus we are justified in concluding that survival of death as disembodied existence in another world is something which we can *conceive*, without contradiction, to be the case. And since we can, we are in a position to look for evidence that such survival is *in fact* the case. It is to this task that we shall now turn.

7

SCIENCE AND
THE PARANORMAL

IF MY ARGUMENTS ARE VALID, THEN WHAT I HAVE ES-
tablished so far is that the survival of the individual person in another world is not only clearly conceivable but
also in harmony with all the definitely known facts about
the relationship between consciousness and the brain. In
other words, survival of death is a genuine possibility,
or, as William James would probably put it, a "living
option."[1] But, of course, though survival is a possibility,
it may be that *in fact* we do not survive. So we must
inquire as to whether there are any empirical facts which
show that some people have survived bodily death, or,
failing this, show that survival is more probable than not.
When we look for such facts, it is obvious that we must
reach into areas not commonly investigated. If there were
such facts and they were commonly known, the survival
hypothesis would not be controversial.

We must look for such facts in reports of occurrences
which are so bizarre, so paradoxical to common sense
that, in the opinion of most people, they simply cannot
happen. Let us call such occurrences "paranormal
events." They are events which science and the common

sense of our time regard as impossible because they are violations of fundamental and apparently well-founded assumptions about the nature of our world. Because of this, it is not surprising that the great majority of scientists simply do not pay attention to reports of the occurrence of paranormal events. Since they are "impossible" in terms of the current materialistic world view, they cannot happen. And if they cannot happen, there is no point in paying attention to the evidence indicating that they do happen. But if one ignores this evidence, he will be reinforced in his belief that they cannot happen. Thus, in this circular fashion, one will find "support" for the view with which he began.

Though the scientific method has proved to be an extraordinarily successful one, it cannot be used to justify such an attitude or procedure on the part of individual scientists. The truly scientific attitude is not characterized by a willingness to accept a particular metaphysical creed (whether materialistic or not) about the nature of the world and then, on the basis of it, make proclamations about what can or cannot be in advance of any investigation. Rather, this attitude consists in an open-mindedness, free from favorable and adverse prejudice, which welcomes all facts, however difficult they may be to reconcile with prevailing beliefs about what can take place in our world. It is an attitude prompted by a passion to know the truth, however inconvenient or unsettling that truth may turn out to be. And if such an attitude leads us to facts which threaten or even destroy the materialistic view of modern science, we certainly need not fear the destruction of science itself. In the words of John Beloff,

> The time has now come, I suggest, when we must rethink the scientific enterprise. Our mistake, it seems to me, is that what, for the past three centuries, we have taken to be distinctive of science,

namely its determinism and materialism, was never its most valuable feature; rather, as Popper has never tired of telling us, what we should be paying attention to is its openness and its fallibilism.[2]

So let us turn to a consideration of paranormal phenomena, free from a paralyzing worry that this area is still ignored by the greater part of the scientific world.

I have already mentioned one group of apparently paranormal events—psi phenomena. They fall into two main categories: psi cognition, better known as extrasensory perception (ESP), and psi action, also known as psychokinesis (PK). ESP can be subdivided into two basic forms depending upon whether the source of information is another mind or a non-mental event or object. These basic forms are: (1) telepathy—a direct communication between minds which takes place independently of the sense organs and irrespective of distance between them or intervening obstacles; and (2) clairvoyance—a detailed and correct virtual perception of things, objects or events which are not accessible to one's sense organs at the time of apprehension. Since ESP seems to be independent of time as well as space, the source of information may be in the future, thus giving rise to *precognitive* telepathy or clairvoyance, or in the past, in which case we would speak of *retrocognitive* telepathy or clairvoyance. PK, on the other hand, is not a means of acquiring information but a means of *acting* on the environment. It is conceived as direct action of mind upon matter, independently of bodily limbs, nerves, and muscles.

Now, though psi phenomena are not directly relevant to the question of whether we shall in fact survive bodily death, they have indirect relevance in at least two respects. To begin with, they can be used to provide an alternative interpretation of apparently paranormal phenomena which would otherwise seem to indicate survival of death. And secondly, the existence of psi strongly supports, if it does not establish, a view of the mind-body relationship in which survival is something we ought to expect. The first consideration is one to which I shall later return. With respect to the second, the existence of psi suggests not only that the mind is distinct from the brain but that it can sometimes function independently of the brain and body. For there is nothing in all of our knowledge of the nature and functioning of the brain which would lead us to believe, or even to suspect, that the brain can sometimes acquire information other than via the nerves and sense organs, or that it can affect the material environment other than by way of the neuro-muscular systems of the body. So if these psi functions occur, it would certainly seem that it is the mind which is responsible for them.

A materialist may object that we really do not have any knowledge which suggests that the mind can do this either. But there is a case for saying that we are really quite ignorant of the potentialities of the mind. Though we know a great deal about matter, and even much about brain matter, we know little about the capacities of the mind. Of course, our knowledge of our own conscious states is unparalleled. They can be known with a certainty that we cannot achieve with respect to material objects or the conscious states of others. But if we suppose, as I think we must, that a mind includes not only the conscious states which we directly apprehend, but also various "powers" or capacities for experience of various kinds, then a considerable portion of the mind turns out to be something which is not directly apprehended and not conscious. We know that we have an abiding capacity to remember, to think, to experience sensations, to imagine, to desire, to feel, to experience emotions, moods and impulses. But we know almost nothing about the full extent of the capacities of the mind and thus are certainly not in a position to say that they could not include a capacity for psi.

Though there are many who still doubt that there are any psi phenomena, this is a doubt that is becoming more and more difficult to maintain. In view of the investigative efforts of the British and American Societies for Psychical Research and parapsychologists such as J.B. Rhine and Charles Tart, it now seems more appropriate to ask not *whether* to believe there are psi phenomena but *how much* to believe. Belief in the existence of ESP has become almost respectable. There seems to be general agreement that telepathy is the best established of the forms of psi with clairvoyance not far behind. Though it would be very convenient to be able to dismiss precognition from further consideration because of the extreme difficulty in making any sense out of it, this cannot be done. For some of the best evidence for telepathy is also evidence for precognition. Psychokinesis, however, is much less well established.

8

OUT-OF-THE-BODY EXPERIENCE

NOW WE WILL TURN TO A CONSIDERATION OF (APPAR-
ently) paranormal phenomena which do seem to have direct relevance to the question of survival. One of the
most interesting kinds is the out-of-the body experience
(OBE). It provides for many people a dramatic but concrete example of what it may be like to exist in a manner
other than in the physical body to which they are accustomed. In its more striking forms, the person concerned
finds himself outside of his physical body, viewing it from
a distance and from a variety of perspectives, just as we
can normally view the body of another. It is as if the self
or person has separated from his physical body and is
now doing his perceiving from a perspective external to
the body. He is often able to view the other contents of
the room from this perspective outside his body and to
observe, and then later describe, the events that took
place while he was "out," even though the body may
have been displaying no signs of consciousness during
this period. He frequently finds himself in another body
(that has been variously termed the secondary body, the
astral body, the etheric body, the spiritual body or the

double) which is apparently non-physical, although it closely resembles the physical body in appearance. That is, he feels that his consciousness is "centered in" this secondary body in the sense in which he ordinarily feels it to be "centered in" his physical body. However, in a few cases, it is not obvious to him that his consciousness is centered in any body at all.

A clear-cut case of an OBE in which consciousness seemed to be centered in a secondary body occurred to Miss M. Hendry of Cleveland, Ohio, who was at the time a graduate nurse. One day when she was assisting a doctor perform an operation in a small country hospital she suddenly seemed to herself to be located behind the doctor, peering over his shoulder watching her physical body which was facing her on the other side of the operating table and engaged in performing the duties of a surgical assistant. She definitely seemed to herself to be located in another body while looking at her physical body across the table and had, at the time, no sense of being in her physical body. She simply viewed the latter from without, as one might view the body of another. When the operation was over she seemed to herself to float up over the table, alight on the other side next to her physical body, and then quickly merge with it.

She had had no warning that the separation was about to take place. She was in good health at the time and was feeling perfectly normal until the moment she noticed that the separation had occurred. Apparently her experience of being out of her body and viewing it from a distance did not interfere with the ability of her body to carry out the duties of a surgical assistant as it continued to perform in such a manner that the doctor noticed nothing odd in its behavior.[1]

Sometimes the out-of-the-body experient finds that he can leave the vicinity of his physical body, travel to distant places, and observe events taking place there more or less as they are actually occurring at the time. Robert

Monroe, a Virginia businessman who reports having had numerous OBEs, describes several of this sort. The following is an interesting example:

In a motel in Winston-Salem: I woke up early and went out to have breakfast at seven-thirty, then returned to my room about eight-thirty and lay down. As I relaxed, the vibrations came and then an impression of movement. Shortly thereafter, I stopped and the first thing I saw was a boy walking along and tossing a baseball in the air and catching it. A quick shift, and I saw a man trying to put something into the back seat of a car, a large sedan. The thing was an awkward-looking device that I interpreted to be a small car with wheels and electric motor. The man twisted and turned the device and finally got it into the back seat of the car and slammed the door. Another quick shift, and I was standing beside a table. There were people sitting around the table, and dishes covered it. One person was dealing what looked like large white playing cards around to the others at the table. I thought it strange to play cards at a table so covered with dishes, and wondered about the overlarge size and whiteness of the cards. Another quick shift, and I was over city streets, about five hundred feet high, looking for "home." Then I spotted the radio tower, and almost instantly I was back in my body. I sat up and looked around. Everything seemed normal.

Important aftermath: The same evening, I visited some friends, Mr. and Mrs. Agnew Bahnson, at their home. They were partially aware of my "activities," and on a sudden hunch, I knew the morning event had to do with them. I asked about their son, and they called him into the room and asked him what he was doing between eight-thirty and nine that morning. He said he was going to school. When asked more specifically what he was doing as he went, he said he was tossing his baseball in the air and catching it. (Although I knew him well,

I had no knowledge that the boy was interested in baseball, although this could be assumed.) Next, I decided to speak about the loading of the car. Mr. Bahnson was astounded. Exactly at that time, he told me, he was loading a Van de Graff generator into the back seat of his car. The generator was a large, awkward device with wheels, an electric motor, and a platform. He showed me the device. (It was eerie to see physically something you had observed only from the Second Body.) Next, I told about the table and the large white cards. His wife was excited at this one. It seems that for the first time in two years, because they had all arisen late, she had brought the morning mail to the breakfast table and had passed out the letters to them as she sorted the mail. Large white playing cards! They were very excited over the event, and I am sure they were not humoring me.[2]

Monroe reports that he had no normal knowledge of these matters and thinks that unconscious preknowledge was unlikely on the grounds that he was unaware of the son's interest in baseball and that activities such as the loading of the Van de Graff generator and the mail sorting at the table were unusual events.

The OBE is not extremely rare. Many who have investigated this phenomenon estimate that about one-quarter of the population have an OBE at some point in their lifetime.[3] Furthermore, it has been occurring at least since the beginning of recorded history. It is frequently a once in a lifetime experience for those to whom it occurs, and it is usually induced by way of illness, accident, anesthesia, or drugs. In the remarkable case of Ed Morrell, the phenomenon was induced by extreme pain. When he was confined in an Arizona prison in the early part of this century, it was standard punishment to wrap intractable prisoners in two straitjackets, one on top of the other, and then cause them to shrink by pouring water on them. When this treatment was applied to Morrell, he found the pain so excruciating that he tried to escape from his predicament by giving up and dying. But instead of dying he suddenly found himself free of his physical body and traveling beyond the prison walls observing events as they were actually taking place. He observed many events which were later verified, one of which involved a shipwreck. This treatment was applied to him repeatedly, but failed to have the usual psychological effect on him, because, instead of being dreadful, it generated a pleasant OBE in which he was entirely free of the pain and physical distress. However, during the latter part of his prison sentence when he was no longer given the straitjacket treatment, he was unable to escape from his prison environment by means of an OBE. He describes his experiences in a book entitled *The Twenty-Fifth Man*.[4]

In some individuals the OBE came to be a rather common experience which, to some extent, they were able to bring under voluntary control. Perhaps the three most important writers in English who have made and elaborated on such claims are Oliver Fox, Sylvan Muldoon, and Robert Monroe. They have had a sufficient amount of OBEs to have learned to keep their heads while having them, and what they have to tell us is based upon a great deal of careful self-observation. Each explains in detail how he first came to have an OBE and how he learned to put himself, more or less at will, into that state. In addition, each provides detailed accounts of numerous OBEs that he has had.

Robert Monroe is able to distinguish three different realms in which he finds himself in his out-of-the-body travels. The first, which he identifies as Locale I or the "Here-Now," consists of people, material objects, and events which actually exist in our world at the moment of the experience. This is the world in which we would expect him to travel, if indeed that is what he does, and the one in which we could verify his out-of-the-body observations by comparing his account of them with what actually took place. However, he claims that he often fails in his efforts to reach Locale I, and that even when he does so he frequently misses the destination which he intends to reach. Instead of reaching Locale I, he may end up in Locale II or III. Locales II and III are unfamiliar to us who inhabit Locale I, but Monroe provides a description of them. He tells us that Locale II is a nonmaterial world, the substance of which is created by thought. Though it contains perceivable objects which seem to be composed of solid matter, they are in fact produced by the consciousness of people who once lived in our physical world and perhaps also, he suggests, by a higher order of intelligent beings because they wish to produce an imitation of the physical environment for the benefit of those people who are just emerging from the physical world after bodily death. It is a vast world, containing all of the features which we attribute to heaven and hell. He claims that most of his attempts to travel out of his body took him involuntarily to this locale because it is the natural environment of the secondary body. By contrast, travel in Locale I is a ''forced'' process which is difficult to bring about, as the secondary body is ''basically not of this physical world.''[5]

Monroe implies that Locale II is a spatial world, but seems puzzled about how to conceive of its location. He tells us that, ''Many theories have been offered in literature throughout the ages as to the ''where'' of it, but few appeal to the modern scientific mind. All of the experimental visits to this area have helped little to formulate a more acceptable theory.''[6] But this is really no problem if, as I suggested earlier, we recognize that a world can be spatial without bearing any spatial relationship to this one, in which case the question of *where* it is in relation to this one does not even arise. We can conceive of reaching such a world not by traveling through a certain amount of physical space, but by a change of consciousness analogous to that which takes place when we dream. Perhaps Monroe would find this quite in agreement with his views; for he goes so far as to assert that, "As can be inferred, I suspect that many, most, or all human beings visit Locale II at some time during the sleep state."[7]

Monroe believes that Locale III is a physical world very similar to our own. He claims that it contains trees, houses, people, cities, railroads, and businesses just as ours does. However, the scientific development is different. There is no electricity, electromagnetics, or electrical devices. And though there is mechanical power, no gasoline, oil, or internal combustion is used as a power source. Monroe claims to have visited this world many times, but found that the inhabitants of that world were unaware of his presence until he temporarily and involuntarily displaced a man there by taking over his body. After this initial displacement, the process became automatic so that whenever he went to Locale III he took over this body. In this manner he began to live an intermittent life there.

Though Monroe believes Locale III to be a physical world, we need not draw that conclusion. If, as I have argued, ordinary perception is representational, then the source or cause of it is not itself perceived. Thus however vivid, uniform, and coherent Monroe's perception of Locale III may be, the unperceived cause of his experience may nevertheless be something other than matter.

NEAR DEATH AND TEMPORARY DEATH OBE

There are cases of people who have had remarkable OBEs while very near death or even while clinically dead, as established by the absence of clinically detectable vital signs. It is obvious that such OBEs have great relevance to the question of survival of death. For if consciousness is either identical with brain activity or distinct from but produced by brain activity, we might expect consciousness to greatly diminish or disappear entirely when the brain is dying. Yet this is frequently not the case. In a very interesting study of the experiences of the dying and the "dead," Raymond Moody cites numerous cases of lucid, detailed, and remarkably veridical experience of people considered dead or on the brink of death. For example, he cites the case of a woman who recalls the following:

> About a year ago, I was admitted to the hospital with heart trouble, and the next morning, lying in the hospital bed, I began to have a very severe pain in my chest. I pushed the button beside the bed to call for the nurses, and they came in and started working on me. I was quite uncomfortable lying on my back so I turned over, and as I did I quit breathing and my heart stopped beating. Just then, I heard the nurses shout, "Code pink! Code pink!" As they were saying this, I could feel myself moving out of my body and sliding down between the mattress and the rail on the side of the bed—actually it seemed as if I went through the rail—on down to the floor. Then, I started rising upward, slowly. On my way up, I saw more nurses come running into the room—there must have been a dozen of them. My doctor happened to be making his rounds in the hospital so they called him and I saw him come in, too. I thought, "I wonder what he's doing here." I drifted on up past the light fixture—I saw it from the side and very distinctly—and then I stopped, floating right below the ceiling, looking down. I felt almost as though I were a piece of paper that someone had blown up to the ceiling.
>
> I watched them reviving me from up there! My body was lying down there stretched out on the bed, in plain view, and they were all standing around it.

I heard one nurse say, "Oh, my God! She's gone!", while another one leaned down to give me mouth-to-mouth resuscitation. I was looking at the back of her head while she did this. I'll never forget the way her hair looked; it was cut kind of short. Just then, I saw them roll this machine in there, and they put the shocks on my chest. When they did, I saw my whole body just jump right up off the bed, and I heard every bone in my body crack and pop. It was the most awful thing!

As I saw them below beating on my chest and rubbing my arms and legs, I thought, "Why are they going to so much trouble? I'm just fine now."[8]

It is of great interest to note that many of the people Moody studied reported that their ability to think, instead of being diminished as we might expect, was considerably improved. As an example, one man told Moody that while he was "dead,"

Things that are not possible now, are then. Your mind is so clear. It's so nice. My mind just took everything down and worked everything out for me the first time, without having to go through it more than once. After a while everything I was experiencing got to where it meant something to me in some way.[9]

Perception, too, is heightened in some respects, even though the physical sense organs are inoperative during the experience. Though kinesthetic sensations and the sensations of taste and smell were absent in the cases that Moody studied, vision and hearing seemed more perfect than in normal experience. Moody quotes one woman as noting that, "It seemed as if this spiritual sense had no limitations, as if I could look anywhere and everywhere." A woman who found herself out of her body after an automobile accident describes such an experience in more detail:

There was a lot of action going on, and people running around the ambulance. And whenever I would look at a person to wonder what they were thinking, it was like a zoom-up, exactly like through a zoom lens, and I was there. But it seemed that part of me—I'll call it my mind—was still where I had been, several yards away from my body. When I wanted to see someone at a distance, it seemed like part of me, kind of like a tracer, would go to that person. And it seemed to me at the time that if something happened anyplace in the world that I could just be there.[10]

It is interesting to note that sensitives or psychics have described their clairvoyant experiences in a similar manner. Eileen Garrett, for example, notes that her clairvoyant experience may include:

. . . a strange picture in which one sees through and beyond barriers that would completely balk our ordinary sensory vision. A road may wind among hills for any distance. One sees the hills, and as the road reaches away, perspective operates and its farther dimensions diminish, as they would diminish to our sight or in any picture. Nevertheless, at the same time, one sees the entire road completely, regardless of the intervening hills, and its farther reaches are as meticulously discernible as the areas that lie close to the spot from which one is seeing. Each rut and stone is individually seen and can be described with precision. The leaves of trees and the blades of grass are countable throughout the landscape. . . . It is more clear to me than it would be were I present on the spot, for I see it all at once, all together in a breath of time, and I do not have to shift the focus of my vision from one part of the picture in order to see it whole, entire, complete.[11]

Telepathy also seems to be involved in the OBE. It may be the process by which a person having an OBE is able to "hear" what is going on around him despite the fact that his ears are apparently inoperative at the time. At any rate, the following description of an OBE suggests that this is sometimes the case:

> I could see people all around, and I could understand what they were saying. I didn't hear them audibly, like I'm hearing you. It was more like knowing what they were thinking, exactly what they were thinking, but only in my mind, not in their actual vocabulary. I would catch it the second before they opened their mouths to speak.[12]

Of course, it will be pointed out that the people whose experiences Moody cites did not really die, even if they were pronounced clinically dead. Since their brain cells did not die, these OBEs certainly do not show that consciousness can exist independently of a living brain. A skeptic might argue that brain cells suffering an unusual deprivation of oxygen may very well generate highly unusual experience. But though such a possibility cannot be ruled out, it seems improbable that brain performance in producing consciousness would remain undiminished, to say nothing of improving, when it undergoes severe oxygen deprivation. On the other hand, such a result is just what we might expect if, as I suggested earlier, the brain functions as a selective-inhibitor of consciousness, restricting attention to what is useful in the struggle for survival. The view that the inhibitor is progressively relaxing as the oxygen deprivation becomes more severe is quite in agreement with Moody's observation that, "In general, persons who were 'dead' seem to report more florid, complete experiences than those who only came close to death, and those who were 'dead' for a longer period go deeper than those who were 'dead' for a shorter time."[13]

Apparent Encounters with the Dead in OBE

Monroe reports having had several OBEs which involved what seemed to him to be encounters with the dead. For example, he reports viewing via an OBE a deceased friend, Dr. Richard Gordon, under conditions which incline one to say that in some sense he really did meet the deceased Dr. Gordon. Monroe did not know Gordon as a young man, having met him for the first time when the latter was in his fifties. At that time Gordon was short and thin, with straight white hair, tending to baldness. Monroe knew Gordon for almost twenty years, and they became close friends. And when Gordon died, Monroe tried to contact him by means of an OBE. He describes his experience as follows:

On a Saturday afternoon, I made the attempt. It took about an hour to get into the vibrational state, and I finally swung up out of the body mentally yelling, I want to see Dr. Gordon!

After a moment, I started to move rapidly upward, and soon all I could see was a blur of motion and feel what seemed like a rush of very thin air. Also, I felt a hand under my left elbow. Somebody was helping me get there.

After what seemed an endless journey, I suddenly stopped (or was halted). I was standing, somewhat dazed, in a large room. My impression was that it was an institution of some kind. The hand under my elbow moved me to an open doorway, and stopped me just inside the door, where I could look into the adjoining room. A male voice spoke almost directly into my left ear.

"If you stand right here, the doctor will see you in a minute."

I nodded agreement, and stood there waiting. A group of men were in the room. Three or four were listening to a young man about twenty-two who was excitedly relating something to them, complete with gestures.

I didn't see Dr. Gordon, and kept expecting him to appear at any moment. The more I waited, the warmer I seemed to feel. Finally, I became so hot that I was extremely uncomfortable. I didn't know what was causing me to feel so hot, and I wasn't sure I could stand it much longer. It actually felt as if streams of perspiration were running down my face. I knew that I couldn't stay much longer; I couldn't take the heat. If Dr. Gordon didn't appear soon, I would have to go back without seeing him.

I turned and looked again at the group of men, thinking that perhaps I should ask them about Dr. Gordon. At just that moment, the short, thin young man with the big shock of hair stopped in the middle of his conversation, and looked at me intently for a moment. After the simple short glance, he turned back to the other men and continued his animated discussion.

The heat became unbearable, and I decided I had to leave. I couldn't wait for Dr. Gordon. Using a motion I had learned, I moved quickly upward and away from the room. It was a long journey back. After reintegrating, I checked my physical body. I felt cold, a little stiff. Certainly there were no streams of perspiration running down my cheeks.

Disappointed, I sat up and made notes of the trip. I had failed for some reason. I had not been able to find Dr. Gordon. Time away from the physical was two hours.

There is a stubborn streak in my heredity. The following Saturday I tried again. Just at the moment I left the physical body and started to yell for Dr.

Gordon, a voice spoke right beside me, almost ir-
ritated.

"Why do you want to see him again? You saw him
last Saturday!"

I was so surprised that I dropped back into the physical almost instantly. I sat up and looked around the
office. There was no one in the room. Everything
was normal. I thought of trying again, but decided
it was too late for another attempt that day.

Last Saturday. There was nothing important about
last Saturday. It hadn't worked. I went back through
my notes for "last Saturday." And there it was.

"The doctor will see you in a minute." And what
could have been a minute later, a short, thin young
man with a shock of hair had turned and looked at
me intently. He had looked at me without saying a
word, as if he were thinking. What I had noted was
a perfect description of what Dr. Gordon would
have been at twenty-two instead of seventy.

This seemed to lend more credence to the experience than anything else. I had expected to see a
man of seventy. I didn't recognize him because he
was not what I expected. If I had suggested this
as hallucination, I conceivably would have met a
seventy-year-old Dr. Gordon.

Later, at a visit to the home of Dr. Gordon's widow,
I managed to see an old photo of Dr. Gordon when
he was twenty-two. Of course, I didn't tell Mrs.
Gordon why I wanted to see the picture. It matched
perfectly the man I saw, and who saw me "there."
She also mentioned that at that age, he was very
active and eager, always in a hurry, and had a big
shock of blond hair.[14]

Monroe describes other apparent encounters of this
sort, including one with his deceased father. Speaking of

their impact upon him he said, "They all led me to an inescapable empirical conclusion, which alone justified the many, many hours of anguish, uncertainty, fear, loneliness, and disillusion. . . ."[15] The conclusion seems to be that "the human personality can and does operate away from the human body" and continues to do so after death.

There is another type of experience closely related to the full-blown OBE which I have been discussing that occasionally involves an apparent encounter with the dead. This is the lucid dream, a dream of a rather peculiar kind which seems to be intermediate between the ordinary dream and the full-blown OBE.

It is a dream in which the dreamer knows that he is dreaming. He clearly remembers his waking life and contrasts it with his present state. He finds that he can think, reason, and direct his attention at will, just as he can when awake. He perceives clearly and can perform experiments on the various objects of his dream environment, just as he might do with the objects of ordinary waking sense perception. His experience of having a body through which he acts upon the objects of his dream is also clear and distinct. But he is also aware of the fact that his physical body is asleep in bed and thus has a different location and posture from the one he is animating in the dream. It may be that the distinction between a lucid dream and an OBE is not completely clear. For lucid dreams, and even ordinary dreams, can be classified as OBEs. Even in the ordinary dream one usually finds himself animating a body which, as one realizes upon awakening, is certainly distinct from the physical body which was asleep in bed during the dream. It is an experience of being in a body other than the physical body, although one does not come to regard it as such until awakening. Now, in the lucid dream this awareness that one is animating a body distinct from one's physical body is present in the dream itself. But the fact that it is nevertheless a *dream* renders it distinguishable from the OBEs which I have been discussing, for these are experiences that one has when *awake*. So even though the lucid dream is characterized by the presence of mind and the perceptual clarity of the waking state, it is nonetheless a dream from which one eventually awakens.

Oliver Fox's out-of-the-body experience begins with a lucid dream (or what he calls a Dream of Knowledge). It is by prolonging such a dream that he learns how to bring about an OBE. Fox finds that such dreams come about when he notices some incongruity in the dream environment which convinces him that he must be dreaming. The following is his account of his first lucid dream—the dream which marked the beginning of his extensive out-of-the-body experience:

> I dreamed that I was standing on the pavement outside my home. The sun was rising behind the Roman wall, and the waters of Bletchingden Bay were sparkling in the morning light. I could see the tall trees at the corner of the road and the top of the old grey tower beyond the Forty Steps. In the magic of the early sunshine the scene was beautiful enough even then. Now the pavement was not of the ordinary type, but consisted of small, bluish-grey rectangular stones, with their long sides at right-angles to the white kerb. I was about to enter the house when, on glancing casually at these stones, my attention became riveted by a passing strange phenomenon, so extraordinary that I could not believe my eyes—they had seemingly all changed their position in the night, and the long sides were now parallel to the kerb! Then the solution flashed upon me: though this glorious summer morning seemed as real as real could be, I was dreaming!

> With the realization of this fact, the quality of the dream changed in a manner very difficult to convey

to one who has not had this experience. Instantly the vividness of life increased a hundredfold. Never had sea and sky and trees shone with such glamorous' beauty; even the commonplace houses seemed alive and mystically beautiful. Never had I felt so absolutely well, so clear-brained, so divinely powerful, so inexpressibly free![16]

Lucid dreams came to be a common occurrence for Dr. F. van Eeden, a Dutch physician. He studied his dreams, keeping a record of the most interesting ones, and recorded several hundred of the lucid kind. In some of the lucid ones, it seemed to him that he was conversing with people whom he knew at the time to be dead. In one lucid dream, after a very pleasant experience of floating in the air over immense brightly colored landscapes, he saw his brother, who had died five years earlier, seated. Van Eeden went up to his brother and said, "Now we are dreaming, both of us." But the brother answered, "No, I am not!"[17] And then van Eeden remembered that his brother had been dead for several years. The two then had a lengthy conversation about the conditions of existence after death, but the brother could or would provide very little information in response to van Eeden's questions.

During the same night in which he seemed to encounter his brother he had a second lucid dream which he describes as follows:

Then a second period of lucidity followed in which I saw Prof. van't Hoff, the famous Dutch chemist, whom I had known as a student, standing in a sort of college-room, surrounded by a number of learned people. I went up to him knowing very well that he was dead, and continued my inquiry about our condition after death. It was a long, quiet conversation, in which I was perfectly aware of the situation.

I asked first why we, lacking our organs of sense, could arrive at any certainty that the person to whom we were talking was really that person and not a subjective illusion. Then van't Hoff said: "Just as in common life; by a general impression."

"Yet," I said, "in common life there is stability of observation and there is consolidation by repeated observation."

"Here also," said van't Hoff. "And the sensation of certainty is the same." Then I had indeed a very strong feeling of certitude that it was really van't Hoff with whom I talked and no subjective illusion. Then I began to inquire again about the clearness, the lucidity, the stability of this life of shades, and then I got the same hesitating, dubious, unsatisfactory answer as from my brother. The whole atmosphere of the dream was happy, bright, elevated, and the persons around van't Hoff seemed sympathetic, though I did not know them.[18]

In another lucid dream, van Eeden had an apparent encounter with his dead brother-in-law. The brother-in-law told of an impending financial catastrophy for van Eeden which seemed to the latter, upon awakening, to be very improbable, but which, in fact, did take place in a very unambiguous manner. Van Eeden also speaks of calling in his lucid dreams for deceased people and claims to have successfully reached them in several cases. He claims to have successfully called his deceased father and various deceased friends and relatives.

It seems appropriate to mention in this context that I have had a few lucid dreams, and that, among other things, they certainly made it clear to me that while asleep I retain the capacity to have vivid and detailed perceptual experience of a world of objects, including one that functions as my body, and all the while to reflect upon what is happening with the presence of mind and the volitional control to which I am accustomed when awake. They provide a sense of another dimension to my experience and a concrete example of how my empirical self may be intimately related to, yet rather effectively insulated from, my transcendental self (if I have one). It is as though I have become a temporary inhabitant of another world which is only a change in consciousness away. And I am astounded, both during the dream and later after awakening, at the vividness and the clarity of the perceptual imagery. When, in a lucid dream, I see the blue sky or the green grass at my feet or the trees along the edge of the field, I see them as clearly, as vividly, and as consciously as I now see the pen in my hand. Then my astonishment intensifies when I reflect upon the fact that all of this is taking place independently of that complex array of external atomic structures, electromagnetic vibrations, retinal stimulation, and sonic waves which bring about my perceptual experience when awake. In the words of van Eeden, "After years of painful study the laws of light and color, and the mechanics of the nervous system were discovered to account for the phenomenon: The sight of a blue sky. And yet there it is again without aether-vibrations, without ocular action; there it is, perfect, vivid, clear, well-observed."[19]

OBE AND THE AFTERLIFE

The OBE and the secondary body have played a prominent role in various cultures and spiritual traditions all around the world. It is of great interest to note that the secondary body is regarded as the body of the self after death. To give a few examples, the ancient Greeks apparently believed that the eidolon, an insubstantial, phantom-like image of the once-living person, continues to exist after death. Homer tells of the shades of the dead which continue to exist in Hades. It seems that ancient

Egyptians believed that a birdlike double of the person leaves the physical body at death. This is presumably what the ''ka''—the birdlike figure depicted in ancient Egyptian frescoes—represents. And we ought not forget St. Paul who, in I Corinthians 15, writes:

> When the body is buried it is mortal; when raised it will be immortal. When buried, it is ugly and weak; when raised, it will be beautiful and strong. When buried, it is a physical body; when raised, it will be a spiritual body. There is, of course, a physical body, so there has to be a spiritual body. For the scripture says: ''The first man, Adam, was created a living being''; but the last Adam is the life-giving spirit. It is not the spiritual that comes first, but the physical, and then the spiritual. The first Adam was made of the dust of the earth; the second Adam came from heaven.[20]

St. Paul's assertion that the spiritual body will be beautiful and strong, even though the physical body may be ugly and weak, is in remarkable agreement with reports of OBEs in which the experient finds his secondary body to be healthy, whole, and intact, even though his physical body is diseased, in pain, mangled and bleeding in a wreckage, or missing one or more limbs. Similarly, the secondary body often appears ageless or youthful even though the physical body is old and decrepit.

One of the most remarkable accounts of the secondary body and its release when death comes is to be found in the Bardo Thödol, known in English as the *Tibetan Book of the Dead*.[21] It was compiled from the teachings of saints and seers over many centuries in prehistoric Tibet and passed along by word of mouth until it was finally written down in about the A.D. 700s. But even then it was sealed with ''the seven seals of silence'' for fear that its knowledge would be misunderstood. It has been hailed as ''one of the most remarkable works the West has ever

received from the East.''[22] And this is not an overstate-
ment if the book is what it claims to be. For it claims to
be a description of the afterlife which is based not upon
mere faith, belief, or tradition, but upon the actual experience of *yogis* who claim to have died and experienced the
conditions of existence after death, and then returned
through the process of rebirth, maintaining all the while
the unbroken continuity of consciousness which enables them to provide us with an accurate account of the
events which transpired. Thus it constitutes a direct challenge to those who are fond of arguing that no one can
speak with authority about death and the conditions which
follow it because no one has had any experience of such
things.

This book professes to describe the stage of existence
between death and rebirth (viz., the Bardo state) and was
read to the dying person in an effort to help him understand and respond appropriately to what was about to
happen to him. It was also read repeatedly after death in
a further effort to help the dead person at a time when
the teaching is desperately needed and readily applied.
These teachings are so detailed and intricately adapted to
the apparent changes in the dead person's condition as he
progresses through the Bardo world that it is difficult not
to seriously ask ourselves whether these wise old *yogis*
and *lamas* might not, after all, have pierced the veil
which hides the greatest of life's mysteries and caught a
glimpse of the existence which lies beyond. And as we
look at this account, which purports to be a description
of an afterlife which actually awaits us, I wish to draw
attention to its remarkable correspondence with the conception of disembodied existence that I presented earlier,
as well as with other accounts of out-of-the-body experience.

When death occurs the mind or consciousness leaves
the body, and soon thereafter the conscious self enters a
''swoon'' which lasts three and one-half days. The newly

dead finds himself still in existence in a non-physical void. He is surprised to find that he is out of his body and can view his corpse as it is being prepared for the funeral rites. He can see and hear his friends and relatives mourning, but, much to his dissatisfaction, they cannot see him or hear him call. He is confused about this, as he does not yet realize that he is dead. He begins to wonder what has happened and finally concludes that he is dead. He is then oppressed with intense sorrow and wonders what he should do.

He has a body which appears to him to be fleshy and to closely resemble his former body, but in fact is not a material body of flesh and blood. Since this body is non-material, he "hast the power to go right through any rock-masses, hills, boulders, earth, houses, and Mt. Meru itself without being impeded."[23] He can arrive instantaneously at any place to which he wishes to travel. This secondary body (variously called the Bardo, the radiant, or the shining body) is endowed with all of the senses. He sees familiar people and places on earth just as we see in dreams. However, these senses are more acute and more perfect than those of the physical body. Furthermore, even if he were crippled, blind, or deaf in the physical body, he will find that his secondary body is not crippled and all of his senses unimpaired and very keen.

The intellect is exceedingly clear in the Bardo state. Thought becomes very lucid and memory is greatly enhanced. Apprehension and recollection are virtually instantaneous. One in the Bardo state is capable of concentrating and meditating on whatever he is taught, however obtuse he may have been in the physical body. Thus instruction is likely to be particularly effective when given to one in this state. Moreover, in addition to possessing all his perceptual and cognitive faculties in a more or less perfect condition, he possesses "supernormal power of perception of a limited kind."[24] That is, he has what we might call a psi capacity which enables him, at least to a limited extent, to see and hear clairvoyantly, to read the thoughts of others, and to precognize the future.

It is of considerable interest to note that the *Bardo Thödol* has a great deal to say about the nature of the secondary body and that this body is of the kind to which I was referring when I contended that a disembodied subject of experience could seem to himself to have a body. It is repeatedly implied in the *Bardo Thödol* that although the secondary body looks very much like the physical body—so much so that the newly deceased has a difficult time realizing that he is dead—it is, in fact, a body of the sort that we experience when we dream. It is called the thought-body, the mental body, and a "thought-form hallucination."[25] It is conceived to be a mind-dependent body generated by the self, utilizing memories and desires carried over from one's experience in the physical body. And not only is the secondary body composed of mental images, but so is every other object of that world.

Another astonishing account of the conditions of life after death is to be found in the writings of Emanuel Swedenborg. Swedenborg was a highly intelligent and extremely learned man. In addition to having great scientific ability, he was also a practical man of affairs who displayed a great deal of practical wisdom in affairs of state as well as in managing his own affairs. But he also claimed to have experiences in which he seemed to himself to leave the physical realm and enter the world of spirits of the dead, to examine that world leisurely, and converse with several of the beings he met there.

Swedenborg claims to have been guided by some of these beings through the experience of dying so that he could come to know what it is like. Separation from the body occurs and is followed by the person awakening in the threshold of the inner spiritual world. Immediately after death a person is dominated by his "outer self," which is that part of his being that deals with other persons and external things. Its role has been so dominant during physical life that one frequently comes to assume that it is the whole of one's being. "External memory" (i.e., the ability to recall features of one's environment) soon becomes very strong—so strong that memories of one's physical existence now appear with the vivid, striking quality of perception. When a person at this stage thinks of another person's physical appearance, that individual seems to him to be physically present before his eyes. Similarly, he will have perceptual-like experiences of a body which he takes to be his own. Thus the newly dead will likely regard himself as still in the physical body, living in the same house, and still doing what he was accustomed to do while in the physical body. Because of this, he may at first have a difficult time realizing that he has gone through the episode of death and physical disembodiment. As Swedenborg says,

> The first state of man after death is like his state in the world, because he is still in like manner in externals. He has therefore a similar face, a similar speech, and a similar disposition . . . so that he knows no other than that he is still in the world, unless he pays attention to the things that he meets with, and to what was said by the angels when he was raised up—that he is now a spirit.[26]

External memory, though vivid, is not subject to much control by a spirit. Spirits often have a difficult time recalling what they want to recall at a given time.[27] But, says Swedenborg, he was often able to help them in their efforts by providing a suitable reminder. Though spirits have at least a temporary limitation in this respect, they have a great ability to tap the memories of others. They have access to the memories of every kind of experience another person has had, whether that person is in the discarnate or the embodied state. Swedenborg claims that they would frequently tap his memories when he was conversing with them.

Swedenborg's remarks about the method of communication employed in the spirit world are of considerable interest. Whereas our language consists in a number of conventional symbols, it seems that the language of the Next World consists in a system of visual images which are conveyed telepathically from mind to mind. When a spirit communicates with a person of this world, the telepathically conveyed ideas and images fall automatically into the appropriate words of that person's native language, just as they do when he gives verbal expression to his own ideas and imagery. It is because of this, Swedenborg explains, that he would hear a spirit speaking to him in Swedish, his native language, even though the spirit could not converse in that language.

Swedenborg mentions that spirits were often confused about the nature of the communication process, claiming that they literally spoke to him in their own native languages and that he heard them with his ears and apparently understood their languages. However, he pointed out to them that they must be mistaken about this because they have no lips or vocal cords to set the air in motion and that without such motion his ears would not receive stimulation. Instead of speaking to him literally they convey ideas telepathically, and these ideas get expressed to him in Swedish words which he hears, not literally, but "in his mind's ear." He adds that the spirits of the recently dead are similarly confused about how they communicate with each other, supposing that they do so by speech. But eventually they come to realize that this is a mistake founded upon the illusion that they still have physical bodies, and that, in reality, they have been communicating by means of telepathically conveyed visual imagery.

INTERPRETATION

What should we make of these reports of people seeming to themselves to leave their physical bodies and sometimes encounter the dead in other worlds? The first point to note is that we are not in a position to deny that people really do have the experience of leaving their bodies and existing apart from them. It is not difficult to admit that such experiences actually occur when we reflect upon the fact that almost all of us have had numerous dreams and that even ordinary dreams may be regarded as low-level OBEs—OBEs in which the degree of self-awareness and autonomy is low. How else can we regard them when we remind ourselves that in our dreams we may be visiting with others, flying through the air, or battling with monsters when all the while our physical bodies are asleep in bed? But they are common and we have learned to live with them. We simply assert that they are "only dreams." Thus we banish them from our minds as effectively as if they had never occurred and, consequently, fail to appreciate their inexplicable strangeness. If they were not so common, we may be obliged to consider them as paranormal as we now regard the full-blown OBE. So the question, then, is not *whether* the experience of being out-of-one's-body actually does occur, but how this experience should be interpreted.

Do such experiences show that the self is separable from the body and capable of existing independently of it? This is the conclusion of many who have had OBE. For example, Giuseppe Costa, after having a dramatic OBE, writes, "I thus had the most evident proof that *my soul had detached itself from my body during its material existence.* I had, in fact, received proof of the existence of the soul and also of its immortality, since it was true that it had freed itself . . . from the material envelope of the body, acting and thinking outside it."[28] But this is certainly not the only possible conclusion. A skeptic might very well argue that an OBE is simply a peculiar kind of hallucination. Instead of hallucinating, say, pink snakes or pink elephants, one hallucinates his own body as being some distance away in his visual field. In other words, the skeptic might continue, the OBE is an experience which is totally subjective, having no objective significance whatsoever. Just as there are no pink snakes, so there is no secondary body. Nor does the self leave the body. It merely seems that way.

It must be emphasized, however, that the people who have had OBE have no doubt about the significance of the experience and object to calling it a hallucination. Consider, for example, the case of a man who had suffered a temporary death as a result of an accident. He writes,

> It was nothing like an hallucination. I have had hallucinations once, when I was given codeine in the hospital. But that had happened long before the accident which really killed me. And this experience was nothing like the hallucinations, nothing like them at all.[29]

The great psychiatrist, C.G. Jung, felt the same way about an OBE that he had during a temporary death as the result of a heart attack: "It was not a product of imagination. The visions and experiences were utterly real; there was nothing subjective about them; they all had the quality of absolute objectivity. . . ."[30]

However, if we are to answer with any clarity the question of whether an OBE is or is not a hallucination, we must define a hallucination more carefully. Apparently, a hallucination is ordinarily regarded as "a false perception in the absence of an external stimulus." On this view, the experience of seeing pink snakes as a result of drinking too much alcohol is a paradigmatic case. It follows from such a definition that a hallucination can never be veridical (i.e., truth disclosing). But, as we have seen, many OBEs involve *accurate* observation of one's own body and of other things from a point of view distant in space from that body. Thus we can hardly say that such observations are *false* perceptions, despite the fact that they do not arise in the way normal perceptions do.

Let us define a hallucination as a mental image of a sensory kind (usually visual, auditory, or tactual) which has the vividness of a perception, but which occurs in the absence of any stimulation from an object of the sort that seems to be perceived. In this definition an OBE would be a hallucination, but the fact that it is would not prevent it from being veridical. For, in this definition, when we say that an OBE is, or is only, a hallucination, we are certainly not explaining either its content or its occurrence. We are merely saying that it is *not* due to stimulation of the relevant sense organ(s) by a physical object of the sort that seems to be perceived.

So whether or not we regard an OBE as a hallucination, we are still left with the fundamental question of how it can be veridical in certain respects. How can a person have a veridical perceptual-like experience of his body and its surroundings from a point of view distant in space from them, or of an environment far from the location of his body, at a time when his physical sense organs are inoperative or not in a position to receive stimulation from the objects seemingly perceived? It is tempting to explain this by concluding, as Costa does, that the observing and thinking consciousness separates from the body and does the perceiving, perhaps by way of the secondary body. But we cannot exclude the possibility that the remarkable information acquired is clairvoyantly apprehended and then construed in consciousness as an OBE. And if this is always the case, then the OBE would not constitute evidence that the self sometimes separates from the body.

Perhaps we can probe a little deeper. When we ask

how someone can have an experience of being "out" of his body we must ask ourselves what we could have had in mind by assuming that he was "in" it in the first place. He is not in it in the sense of being identical with it. For, as we have seen, we must distinguish between the conscious self and the body. Nor is it plausible to hold that he is in his body in a spatial sense; for consciousness is not in space. He may find himself in a secondary body which is in space. But he need not be identified with the secondary body either. However, even if he were to be so identified, he ought not be considered as spatially in the physical body. For it seems that the secondary body is best understood as an image body, and such a body need not bear any spatial relationship to the physical body.

I suggest that a person is in his body only in the sense of being intimately related to it. He is so entangled in his bodily existence that he frequently regards himself as identical with his bodily organism. But this is to say that he is already out of his body in the sense that his being as a conscious self is logically distinct from it. As we have seen, the conscious self and the body are different things, however closely connected they are.

However, there is a more radical sense in which a person may be regarded as already "out" of his body. I suggest that instead of regarding the center of consciousness as "in" the body and sometimes managing in a paranormal manner to get "out," it is more in agreement with the truth to suppose that the body is "in" the field of consciousness.[31] According to the representative theory of perception, the body which we perceive is, as we have seen, a set of percepts or images caused to arise in our experience due to stimulations of the brain by the physical body. The body which I see, touch, feel, and regard as mine should, I suggest, be regarded as a set of persistent visual, tactile, and other percepts which constitute the center of my perceptual world. This set of percepts is organized in such a way as to constitute an object which endures through time and which is one of the objects in my field of consciousness. Thus it is in my field of consciousness, just as the body that I sometimes dream that I have is in my field of consciousness.

The findings of parapsychology also provide support for the view that my body is in my consciousness by indicating that the reach of consciousness extends in both space and time beyond the sphere of my bodily organism's functioning. As we have seen when we considered the existence of various psi capacities, it seems that the field of consciousness is sometimes affected by objects and events which have no physical contact whatsoever with the brain or body. Furthermore, there is evidence that altered states of consciousness activate this extended psi-field of functioning and provide experiences which suggest that consciousness is enhanced in certain respects when the body gets out of its way, so to speak. As we have noted, Aldous Huxley suggests, on the basis of his experience with mescaline, that the brain is a reducing valve, restricting consciousness to what is likely to be practically useful. And when that valve is impaired by the action of certain drugs, or, perhaps, by meditation or certain kinds of exercises, various biologically useless things begin to happen. Extrasensory perception may occur or even a mystical experience of the sort that Huxley had while under the influence of mescaline. But if the body, with its brain and sensory systems, restricts the range of consciousness as Huxley and others claim, then an OBE should be understood not as a case of getting out of the body, but of the body getting out of the way of consciousness.

The physical body (composed of molecules, atoms, force-fields, etc.) plays a causal role in the generation of my experience of my body, but it is epistemologically remote. I do not directly apprehend my physical body. Rather, I infer its existence. It is not on the level of direct experience. On that level, my body is an organized set of percepts, not the cause or explanation of them.

From this perspective, an OBE can be understood as a mere shift from the usual position of one of the objects in a person's field of consciousness. Admittedly, the object whose position has shifted has a unique and very important position in the field of consciousness. For its location and posture ordinarily determine the perspective from which I do my perceiving. It is because of this that I may feel myself to be located in my body, and, consequently, that I must get out to view it from a distance. But if an OBE is to be construed simply as an experience characterized by a change in the relationship between the perspective from which I am perceiving and the location of one of the objects (viz., my body) in my field of consciousness (which includes many other objects of perception as well), there would be no need to suppose that I must get out of my body to have such an experience. Being out of it would be the normal state of affairs. And if this is the normal state of affairs, then surviving the death of the body would not be surprising.[32]

9

DEATH-BED EXPERIENCES

CERTAIN EXPERIENCES WHICH NUMEROUS PEOPLE HAVE had at the threshold of death provide further evidence of a life after death. Many people who were clearly conscious while dying claimed to have received a glimpse of an afterlife in another world and have been able to report what they experienced before dying. They see and sometimes converse with apparitions of deceased friends and relatives whose apparent purpose is to take the dying person away to another mode of existence. They sometimes experience non-earthly and brightly illuminated landscapes of great beauty and intense color. These experiences are accepted as real without question. Only in very rare cases does the person doubt what he sees. They have a transforming effect upon his feelings. They bring peace of mind, serenity, and even elation. The person dies in an elevated mood which is in striking contrast to the misery and gloom that are commonly expected to prevail at the time of death.

Some of the most remarkable death-bed visions are those which have been called "Peak in Darien" experiences. In such an experience, the dying person "sees," usually in company with other deceased relatives or friends waiting to welcome him to the afterlife, a person whom he did not know was dead. He expresses the appropriate emotional reaction of surprise, disbelief, and even shock, at seeing such a person among the deceased. Sir William Barrett reports a very interesting case of this sort in his book, *Death-Bed Visions*. Barrett's wife, a physician, had been called in to deliver the child of a woman named Doris, and although the child was delivered safely, Doris herself was dying. Lady Barrett describes Doris' experiences during her final moments:

> Suddenly she looked eagerly towards one part of the room, a radiant smile illuminating her whole countenance. "Oh, lovely, lovely," she said. I asked, "What is lovely?" "What I *see*," she replied in low intense tones. "What do you see?" "Lovely brightness—wonderful beings." It is difficult to describe the sense of reality conveyed by her intense absorption in the vision. Then— seeming to focus her attention more intently on one place for a moment—she exclaimed, almost with a kind of joyous cry, "Why, it's Father! Oh, he's so glad I'm coming; he *is* so glad. It would be perfect if only W. (her husband) would come too."
>
> Her baby was brought for her to see. She looked at it with interest, and then said, "Do you think I ought to stay for baby's sake?" Then turning towards the vision again, she said, "I can't—I can't stay; if you could see what I do, you would know I can't stay."[1]

Apparently the vision was so real and so irresistible to the young woman that she was willing to give up her life and her baby. Of course, one must consider the view that the vision was simply the product of her dying brain as it attempted to alleviate severe stress and fear of dying by means of a gratifying vision. Barrett considered such a view and then rejected it, mainly because of the fact that among the apparitions of the dead seen by Doris was that of her sister, Vida, who had died about three weeks earlier. Vida's death had not been revealed to Doris because of her precarious condition. Thus it is understandable that Doris was surprised when Vida appeared with her deceased father:

> She spoke to her father, saying, "I am coming," turning at the same time to look at me, saying, "Oh, he is so near." On looking at the same place again, she said with a rather puzzled expression, "He has Vida with him," turning again to me saying, "Vida is with him!"[2]

She died shortly afterwards.

Barrett was so impressed by the apparition of Vida that he began the first systematic study of cases of this kind which resulted in his book, *Death-Bed Visions*. He found that death-bed visions frequently occur when the mind is clear, rational, and well-oriented. In such visions, the dying often see deceased persons who have come to take them away to another mode of existence. Furthermore, what they see is sometimes surprising to them, as it does not agree with their expectations. Though most death-bed visions are seen only by the dying person, Barrett reports a few cases in which a relative or nurse who was present also saw the vision.

There have been more recent studies of death-bed experiences which utilized modern survey methods and computer analysis of results not available to Barrett. In 1959-60, Dr. Karlis Osis, a respected parapsychologist, conducted a mass survey in which he asked thousands of doctors and nurses in the United States about the death-bed visions of their patients.[3] This pilot survey, as it was called, resulted in 640 replies which were based on observations of over 35,000 dying patients. Many of the people who responded were interviewed in great depth, and, as a result, data sufficient for a valid scientific analysis were obtained. The pilot study, which largely confirmed the findings of Barrett, was followed by two more surveys: (1) another United States survey conducted by Osis in 1961-64,[4] and (2) an Indian survey conducted by Osis and E. Haraldsson in 1972-73.[5]

Before looking at what these studies reveal about the nature and conditions of death-bed visions, it may be well to remind ourselves that such experiences are subject to two very different interpretations. The one view (viz., the survival hypothesis) is that these experiences (or, at least, some of them) are just what they appear to be— evidence that death is a transition to another mode of existence. The other is that death constitutes the complete destruction of the person and that a death-bed vision is either the result of a malfunction of the dying brain or a psychological escape into a world of fantasy to alleviate the fear, the pain, and the severe stress involved in dying. Of course, the content of death-bed visions cannot be directly verified as memories and perceptions can be. We obviously cannot proceed to the afterworld to check for correspondence between the content of the vision and some feature of that world. However, there are other nondirect, circumferential ways of determining whether a death-bed experience is veridical which have been used with success in science. The astronomer, for example, is not in a position to directly observe the galaxies and clusters of stars that he studies. Since many are millions of light years away he must be content to analyze the light which left them millions of years ago and make very indirect inferences about their present behavior and location. Yet this has not prevented the science of astronomy from making some astounding breakthroughs. Similarly, as Osis and Haraldsson point out, we must look for indirect evidence which may have some bearing on the veridical nature of death-bed experiences.

One remarkable finding emerging from all three studies is that the hallucinatory experiences of the dying (i.e., death-bed visions) mainly portray otherworldly messengers—usually apparitions of dead relatives. On the other hand, only a small minority of the hallucinations in the general population portray such things. More specifically, all three surveys revealed that the people who were dying saw afterlife-related apparitions of the dead three times as frequently as did people in normal health. Osis and Haraldsson emphasize this point: "This finding is loud and clear: *When the dying see apparitions, they are nearly always experienced as messengers from a postmortem mode of existence.*"[6]

Secondly, the three surveys were in agreement in what they indicated about the apparent main purpose of the apparition portrayed in death-bed visions. It is to take the dying person away to another mode of existence. The apparition expressed a take-away purpose in three out of four cases involved in the surveys. Such a purpose is just what one might expect to find if the survival hypothesis were true. If there is an afterlife, then we ought not find it surprising to find the deceased assisting someone who is dying to make the transition to their mode of existence. The survival hypothesis gains further support in the fact that the vast majority of the persons seen in visions of the dying were deceased close relatives (most commonly, a deceased mother or spouse). For if the deceased continue to exist in another world, it would seem appropriate that our close relatives should be the ones to guide us in making the transition to the afterlife. They would be the ones likely to have the most concern.

The relationship between the appearance of the take-away apparition and the time of death is also what we might have expected on the view that the dying are coming into actual contact with the deceased. For the surveys revealed that when the apparent purpose of the apparition was to take the dying person away to another existence death came more quickly than in those cases where the apparition expressed a different purpose. Even more remarkable and supportive of the survival view is the fact that, in a significant number of cases, the person died in accordance with the "call" of the apparition even when the medical prognosis was recovery.

> Especially dramatic were those cases in which apparitions called a patient for transition to the other world, and the patient, not willing to go, cried out for help or tried to hide. Fifty-four of these "no-consent" cases were observed, nearly all in India. Such cases can hardly be interpreted as projected wish-fulfillment imagery, and they are even more impressive when the apparition's prediction of death was not only correct but contradictory to the medical prognosis of recovery.[7]

In some of the cases included in the surveys, the apparition seen was of someone still living. It is obvious that such cases do not support the survival hypothesis. But it is quite amazing that Osis and Haraldsson did not find a single case in which an apparition of the living portrayed a take-away purpose! And this fact that the take-away purpose was attributed only to apparitions of the dead is certainly in agreement with the view that the dying are actually coming into contact with the dead when they experience the take-away apparition.

What the surveys revealed about the emotional responses of the dying after having seen an otherworldly apparition with a take-away purpose is, at least at first glance, rather surprising. Dying is generally regarded as a time of great sorrow, a time to weep. It is a time of great sadness for family, relatives, and friends, and a fearful time for the one who is dying. But nearly all of the American patients and two-thirds of the Indian patients wanted to go (i.e., to die) after having the death-bed vision. Indeed, in some the desire to go was so strong that they bitterly reproached those who successfully brought them back. Apparently the encounter with the otherworldly apparition was so irresistibly appealing that it completely overshadowed their reasons for living. Their mood changed dramatically before dying. Instead of manifesting the general misery, pain, and depression characteristic of very sick patients, many (49%) became serene, and some (27%) even became cheerful and elated. Many became less agitated, more cooperative, and more communicative. Some who had been in severe pain did not feel pain or discomfort any longer. The case of a stroke patient cited by Osis and Haraldsson is a good example:

> He suddenly didn't want any sedation. He didn't seem to need it. He didn't seem to be in any more pain and was perfectly relaxed; up to this point he had been in severe pain. Blood pressure, pulse stabilized.[8]

The following case of a stroke patient who was partially paralyzed and depressed is a good illustration of the mood change often resulting from a death-bed vision:

> Suddenly his face lit up, pain gone, smiling—he hadn't been cheerful until then. He said, "How beautiful," as if he could see something we couldn't see. And then, "No body, no world, flowers, light and my Mary (deceased wife)." He was released and peaceful, went into a coma and died shortly after.[9]

Though such positive responses may seem surprising, they are really what might be expected on the survival hypothesis. If the dying are actually coming into contact with another world, then serenity, peace, religious emotions, and otherworldly feelings would not be surprising. Responding to otherworldly messengers with otherworldly feelings would be quite appropriate. The presence of such feelings as the ''peace which passeth all understanding'' would be in general agreement with those the mystic reports upon encountering what he regards as transcendental or ultimate reality. Also in accordance with the survival hypothesis is the fact that persons who saw apparitions concerned with this-world purposes, or hallucinated this-world scenery, seldom experienced elation, serenity, peace, or religious emotion.

A more detailed look at the data provided by the surveys lends further support to the survival hypothesis. Among other things to be considered in assessing the significance of death-bed visions are medical factors such as the presence of hallucinogenic drugs and brain disturbances caused by injury, disease, or uremic poisoning (resulting from kidney malfunctioning). In view of the fact that Demerol, morphine, and other powerful hallucinogenic drugs are often administered to the dying in order to alleviate their pain, it may be supposed that the visions are drug-induced. But this supposition is not in accord with the facts. Of the patients who had death-bed visions, only a small minority had received such drugs. And those who had received such drugs did not experience otherworldly apparitions with any more frequency than the others. Thus these studies provide no evidence that drugs produce death-bed experiences suggestive of an afterlife. The same conclusion applies to brain disturbances caused by injury, disease, or uremic poisoning. Such things either *reduced* the frequency of afterlife-related phenomena or else did not affect it at all. The majority of the patients were in a normal, wakeful state of consciousness when the death-bed visions took place. They were not drugged or delirious, but sane and lucid. Thus the medical data provide no support for the view that these visions stem from the malfunction of a sick brain.

There was also no evidence that medical factors caused

the mood elevation and feelings of serenity and peace characteristic of patients who had afterlife-related visions. On the contrary, brain disorders and uremia seem to suppress such mood elevation. There was some evidence that otherworldly visions are suppressed by medical factors which hinder communication with the external world. And this is just what we might expect to find if such visions were due to actual contact with another world.

Another matter to be considered is the role of psychological factors which are known to facilitate hallucinations. Perhaps they bring about the afterlife-related death-bed visions. More specifically, the vision may be a defensive reaction to alleviate the severe stress and the pain often experienced by terminal patients. It may be a product of the patient's desires, an effect of wishful thinking of the sort that causes a thirsty traveler to hallucinate the water that he desperately wants. Or it may be brought about by the patient's expectations. If he expects to die, indulging in otherworldly fantasy may be very comforting and reduce the fear of death. But again the data do not support such speculations. Evidence of anxiety and stress had no influence on the frequency of afterlife-related visions. Nor did the patients see in these visions the people that they had expressed a desire to see. Moreover, a patient's expectations were not any more reliable in predicting the content of his visions. Takeaway apparitions also appeared to those who expected to recover. There was no significant relationship between expectations of the patients and the purpose of the apparition. In many cases the apparition seemed to display a purpose of its own, contrary to the intention of the patient. Such features of death-bed visions suggest that they are not mere subjective creations of the patient's mind, but independent entities with which he is coming into contact.

The fact that one of the studies is of dying persons in

India enables us to examine the role of cultural factors in producing death-bed visions and to consider the question of the objective reality of such visions from yet another perspective. If these visions are produced by what one has acquired from his culture (such as religious and societal beliefs), then they would be fantasies with no objective reality. Consequently, we would expect them to vary a great deal from culture to culture. On the other hand, we would expect them to be essentially the same if they are instances of contact with another mode of existence. There would be some difference due to the influence of culture, but the fundamental characteristics of the phenomena seen in the visions would be essentially the same. And this was the case. Osis and Haraldsson say, *"the similarities between the core phenomena found in the death-bed visions of both countries are clear enough to be considered as supportive of the postmortem survival hypothesis."*[10]

It is apparent, then, that afterlife-related death-bed visions are very remarkable phenomena which cannot be simply brushed aside as the fantasy of very sick, frightened people. Rather, it seems that they receive the best explanation in terms of the survival hypothesis. On that hypothesis alone, the various facts which emerge from a careful analysis of the data fall neatly into place.

I have previously argued that the self must be distinguished from the body and that we can conceive of its surviving apart from the body in another world or mode of existence. And now we see that otherwordly death-bed visions constitute another important piece of evidence that this is *in fact* what happens. When the patient, after experiencing the otherworldly vision, does not feel the pain and discomfort any longer and becomes serene or elated, it is as though the process of disengaging the self from the body has begun. It is as though the connection between the self and the bodily processes is loosening as death approaches, as if in preparation for the transition to another world. If this is the case, we might expect awareness of bodily sensations to diminish. This has happened in many cases. The following is an example of a cancer patient released from excruciating pain:

> The thing that brought it to my attention was that he hadn't had any Demerol for 24 hours. This was a departure from his previous pattern. He said he didn't need any drugs because his pain was gone and he was feeling better. He went into a coma and died within a day.[11]

Of course, other interpretations are possible. Perhaps we are witnessing the dissociation of the personality, the disintegration of the self. However, there are many cases which go against such an interpretation—cases in which the release from pain is conjoined with wholesome, positive changes in the patient and not at all suggestive of disintegration. Among the cases encountered by Osis are two of chronic psychotics who, after having been completely out of touch with reality, returned to their normal selves shortly before death. Perhaps the most interesting cases of this sort are those in which the patient, although dying of a disease which is primarily destructive to the brain, became lucid and normal shortly before death. Such is the case of a woman, dying of meningitis, and severely disoriented almost until the end. But then, "she cleared up, answered questions, smiled, was slightly elated and just a few minutes before death, came to herself. Before that she was disoriented, drowsy, and talked incoherently."[12] It is as if in preparation for the transition her consciousness was becoming disengaged from her brain and, consequently, ceasing to be affected by its malfunctioning.

It is interesting to note that Osis and Haraldsson make sense out of their findings by supposing that the dying become aware of an afterlife by means of ESP. They defend this supposition by pointing to features of death-bed visions which are common to ESP processes. Research on ESP processes outside the field of survival indicates that ESP experiences are usually brief. And, in general, death-bed phenomena suggestive of an afterlife are of shorter duration than those concerned with this life. This is what we would expect to find if the dying were becoming aware of an afterlife by way of ESP. Moreover, the mood elevation can be understood as a result of of extrasensory apprehension of an approaching afterlife. Mood elevation near death resembles those ESP cases in which a person finds himself with feelings which are an appropriate response to the occurrence of a certain event even though he has no conscious knowledge that the event actually occurred. For example, a mother feels very depressed at the time her son is killed in action even though she is not consciously informed of the unfortunate event until later. Similarly, dying patients felt serene or even elated for no apparent reason. They frequently tried to understand this by interpreting it as a sign of recovery, though this proved to be a mistake. But it is what we might expect if it were based on extrasensory apprehension of an approaching afterlife which they find appealing.

The evidence that the dying apprehend an approaching afterlife is in complete accord with the conception of a person and of the afterlife which I presented earlier. Not only does it support the view that there *is* an afterlife, but it is in agreement with the kind of afterlife that I was suggesting. As will be recalled, I have argued that it is conceivable and perhaps even plausible to suppose that a discarnate person apprehends an environment and communicates with others by means of ESP. Furthermore, I advanced various reasons for thinking that ESP would be more prevalent or, at any rate, more apparent when the influence of the brain diminishes and then ceases altogether. So whatever evidence there is for thinking that the dying are apprehending an approaching afterlife by means of ESP is obviously very congenial to the views that I advanced earlier.

10

APPARITIONS AND HAUNTINGS

ANOTHER PHENOMENON WHICH IS SOMETIMES VERY suggestive of survival is the apparition. It is a hallucination in the previously defined sense because no physical object of the kind which seems to be perceived is stimulating the appropriate sense organs at the time of the experience. The kinds of apparitions most relevant to our inquiry are those which appear to be of the dead and which are veridical in that they supply information which was unknown to the percipient. An interesting case is reported by the famous psychic Eileen Garrett. She writes:

> On release from the hospital, I was taken back to my apartment, in order to recuperate. .... I cannot tell you what woke me. I know only that I awoke, and, I looked across the room, expecting to see the nurse sitting in the armchair. I remember looking away and looking back, thinking to myself, "That isn't the nurse!" I did not see a figure then, but I saw hands being extended towards the gas fire. As I looked at the hands, I could see the blood circulating through them, and on the little finger of the

right hand there was a ring, and on it the initials E.H.D. The initials immediately seemed to stand out, to focus my attention.

I then withdrew my gaze from the initials and looked at the feet extending beyond the chair on the floor. They were not the feet of the nurse. They were a man's feet, in evening slippers. He wore two pairs of socks, black over red, as though to keep his feet warm. Then I saw the man, bending forward a little, and looking at me sideways, where I lay in my bed. I saw then that he was dressed, and that he wore two coats: a kind of smoking jacket, and over this a light overcoat. He looked pale and worn, about fifty; he was good-looking with a thin mustache and very blue eyes in a gaunt face. He looked very ill. His hair was fairish, and receding. He was thin about the neck.

As I looked I heard him cough, and he hit his chest and said to me:

"You see what it has done to me. It will also kill you if you remain here. This damp place is over an arm of the canal, and it throws off 'telluric' rays which will undoubtedly make you ill."

He then got up slowly, in a kind of creaking manner, resting heavily on the arms of the chair. I saw him fullface as he looked at me. Then with deliberation he walked out of the open doorway.

When this strange man had gone out into the passage, only then did I realize that something abnormal had occurred. I told Dr. Young when he called later that morning. As I told him the story and described the man to him, he exclaimed, "By God! That is my old patient who died three months ago. If I may have your permission, I would like to tell his widow." This lady came to see me, and told me that her husband—the previous tenant—did die, having had bronchial asthma for a long time; that the ring on his finger had been removed before he died and was now in her possession.

I asked Dr. Young if he had known that the house was built on swampy soil and he said, ''No.'' I do not think I had ever thought very much about the rivers of London until this happened; but then I made a study of them and found that there was indeed a delta under the house.[1]

It is important to note that Mrs. Garrett is certain of being awake while she saw the apparition and heard it speak. Certainty of being awake while viewing the apparition is a feature of experiences of this kind and is one which helps to make them so astonishing. Mrs. Garrett herself is bewildered by them, even though she has had psychic experiences all of her life.

Some experiences of apparitions are very dramatic, preventing the percipient from making a serious mistake or even saving his life. Louisa Rhine cites the case of Norman, an American soldier serving in World War II, whose life was saved because of information he received by way of an apparition of his friend who had been killed about three weeks earlier. Norman was well acquainted with a soldier named Pete and knew that Pete had recently been killed. About three weeks after Pete's death, Norman had driven several staff officers to an outpost behind the front lines on an observation tour. While waiting for them at the outpost, one of the Marines there told him about a shortcut that he could take on the way back. He reached the turning-off place about dusk and turned off onto the shortcut, but had gone only a few feet when he saw Pete about fifty feet ahead in the middle of the road with arms raised as if signaling him to get back on the other road again. So Norman backed his truck out carefully so as to avoid hitting a truckload of marines who were waiting to take the shortcut. The staff officers didn't seem to notice his erratic driving, and so he didn't offer any explanation. It wasn't until he was back on the other road that he suddenly realized that Pete had been dead for some time. The next morning when the casualty reports came in he learned that the truckload of marines which had waited for him as he was backing up had struck a land mine about two miles up the shortcut and that every man had been killed.[2]

Some apparitional experiences are so well attested, so remarkable and clearcut that they have become classics in this area. Such is the case of a traveling salesman's vision of his sister who had been dead for nine years. The experience occurred in St. Joseph, Missouri, where he had been visiting in order to solicit orders for his firm. The trip had been a very successful one, and he was in a cheerful state of mind as he sat at the table in his hotel room, writing up the many orders that he had received. It was noon, the sun was shining brightly, and he was smoking a cigar, absorbed in his business matters, when, as he puts it,

I suddenly became conscious that some one was sitting on my left, with one arm resting on the table. Quick as a flash I turned and distinctly saw the form of my dead sister, and for a brief second or so looked her squarely in the face; and so sure was I that it was she, that I sprang forward in delight, calling her by name, and, as I did so, the apparition instantly vanished. Naturally I was startled and dumbfounded, almost doubting my senses; but the cigar in my mouth, and pen in hand, with the ink still moist on my letter, I satisfied myself I had not been dreaming and was wide awake. I was near enough to touch her, had it been a physical possibility, and noted her features, expression, and details of dress, etc. She appeared as if alive. Her eyes looked kindly and perfectly natural into mine. Her skin was so life-like that I could see the glow or moisture on its surface, and, on the whole, there was no change in her appearance, otherwise than when alive.[3]

From his position at the table he could see the figure clearly from the waist upwards. He had time to notice a comb in her hair and a little breast-pin. She was dressed in clothing she had worn during her lifetime and looked exactly as he had known her when she was alive and well, except for one thing—on the right side of the girl's nose was a bright red scratch about three-fourths of an inch long.

He was so impressed by this experience that he cut short his trip, which would otherwise have lasted for a month, and quickly returned to his parents' home in St. Louis where he related the incident to his parents and other people. When he mentioned the scratch, his mother was profoundly affected and nearly fainted. In his words,

> When I mentioned this my mother rose trembling to her feet and nearly fainted away, and as soon as she sufficiently recovered her self-possession, with tears streaming down her face, she exclaimed that I had indeed seen my sister, as no living mortal but herself was aware of that scratch, which she had accidently made while doing some little act of kindness after my sister's death. She said she well remembered how pained she was to think she should have, unintentionally, marred the features of her dead daughter, and that unknown to all, how she had carefully obliterated all traces of the slight scratch with the aid of powder, &c., and that she had never mentioned it to a human being from that day to this. In proof, neither my father nor any of our family had detected it, and positively were unaware of the incident, yet I saw the scratch as bright as if just made.[4]

What should we make of such experiences? Certainly they must be distinguished from ordinary hallucinations caused by drugs, insanity, delirium, or hypnosis. For they provide the percipient with accurate information which, it would seem, he could not have acquired in any normal way. Perhaps such experiences would not be quite so surprising if they had occurred during a dream, but it seems clear that these percipients were awake. We may think of autosuggestion or vivid imagination, but this is rendered implausible by the fact that the percipients were not even thinking about the deceased people they ostensibly saw. Eileen Garrett had never even seen the man whose apparition appeared to her. And even if something akin to imagination were at work here, this would still not account for the veridical nature of the experiences. Thus it is tempting to conclude that such apparitions are just what they seem to be—instances in which the deceased, who have managed to survive death in some degree or manner, succeed in appearing to, and perhaps communicating with, the living.

However, we must not ignore the possibility of extrasensory perception at work here. Since the information communicated in these cases was known at the time by other living persons, it is certainly conceivable that some sort of telepathic transfer of information from one living person to another is the underlying cause of the experiences. The telepathically acquired information reaches the subliminal mind of the percipient and then gets construed in his consciousness in the form of an apparition. This hypothesis is supported by the fact that there are many cases on record of the percipient viewing an apparition of someone who is still alive. Since such apparitions obviously do not emanate from the dead, it may be that none do. Applying this hypothesis to the case of the salesman, we note that since the mother knew about the scratch, this information could have been communicated telepathically from mother to son. The apparition of the dead sister is the form in which the telepathically acquired information gets interpreted in consciousness.

Though telepathy between mother and son (or other close relatives) does not seem implausible, it is puzzling that nine years elapsed before the telepathic message reached the consciousness of the son. And in the case of the soldiers, if Norman acquired the information telepathically, he must have received it from the minds of the Japanese soldiers who planted the mine. Though this seems unlikely, it is conceivable. The possibility of telepathy from the living cannot be ruled out in these cases. But suppose there were cases in which the information acquired was not known by any living person at the time of the apparitional experience. Such cases would constitute more powerful evidence for survival. Perhaps the most famous case of this sort is the one concerning James Chaffin's will, in which information received via the apparition of a dead man resulted in the discovery of a second will and in a legal judgment setting aside the first one.[5]

It is not clear whether the experiences occurred in a vivid dream or in a waking hallucination. Though an apparition is often regarded as an experience which occurs when one is awake, these experiences, even if they were vivid dreams, should not be discounted for that reason. How we classify them will not affect their weight as evidence for survival.

This case is a very well attested one. A Mr. J. Johnson, a lawyer who was instructed by a member of the Society for Psychical Research (S.P.R.) to investigate on the spot, did so and did a very thorough job. He later submitted to the S.P.R. (1) the original newspaper article about the case, (2) sworn statements of his interviews with the principle members involved in the case in addition to sworn statements by two of them, and (3) the official records of the proceedings of the Superior Court of Davie County, North Carolina.

The essential facts are as follows. James L. Chaffin was a farmer in Davie County, North Carolina. He had a wife and four sons. On November 16, 1905, he made a will attested by two witnesses in which he left his farm to his third son, Marshall, and nothing to the other three or to his wife. However, on January 10, 1919, he made a new will in which he requested that his property be divided equally among his four sons and that they must take care of their mother. He states in the preamble that he was moved to make this new will after reading the twenty-seventh chapter of Genesis (which contains the story of how Jacob deceives his blind father, Isaac, and thereby dishonestly obtains what was meant for the first-born Esau). This will was not witnessed, but it was legally valid because totally in his own handwriting. He placed this will between the two pages containing Genesis 27 of a family Bible which formerly belonged to his father. He folded the pages to form a kind of envelope. So far as can be ascertained, he never told anyone about the existence of his second will, but (as was later discovered) he did secretly stitch a little roll of paper in the inside pocket of his old black overcoat on which he wrote the words: "Read the 27th chapter of Genesis in my daddie's old Bible."

He died on September 7, 1921, as the result of a fall. The sole heir, Marshall, had the first will probated on the 24th of the same month. It was not contested by his wife or his other three sons since they knew of no grounds for doing so. The matter was apparently settled. But almost four years later, in June of 1925, the second son, James Pinkney Chaffin, began to have some very vivid dreams or waking hallucinations (it seems that James himself was uncertain as to which they were) in which his father appeared to him at his bedside without speaking. Later on that month the father appeared again, wearing his familiar black overcoat, and this time spoke, as he pulled back the overcoat, saying, "You will find my will in my overcoat pocket." James looked for the coat the next morning at his mother's house, but she told him that she had given it to his brother, John, who lived about twenty miles away. A few days later James went to his brother's house and found the coat. On examining it, he found that the lining of the inside pocket had been stitched together, and after cutting the stitches he found the little roll of paper on which, in his father's handwriting, was the note about reading the 27th chapter of Genesis in the old family Bible.

At this point James apparently suspected that he was on to something and very wisely decided to get some witnesses to accompany him in his search for his grandfather's Bible. So he returned to his mother's house with his daughter, his neighbor, and his neighbor's daughter. They had some trouble finding the old Bible, and when they finally did, it fell apart. The neighbor picked up the section which happened to contain the book of Genesis, and when he opened it to that book he found the will folded into the pages of chapter 27.

Though the will was not witnessed, it would be legally valid under the laws of North Carolina if it could be shown to the satisfaction of the court that it really was in old Chaffin's handwriting. Marshall Chaffin, the sole heir under the old will, was no longer living, but his widow and son were prepared to contest the new will when the case came before the Superior Court of Davie County in December of 1925. Ten witnesses were present to testify that the will was in old Chaffin's handwriting. But their testimony was not needed. For the widow and son readily admitted this when, during a recess period, they were shown the second will. So the first will was cancelled and the case settled in a friendly manner.

Does this case show that old Chaffin survived death and managed to communicate a message to the living? It is tempting to draw such a conclusion, but first let us consider some other explanations. Perhaps James P. Chaffin planted the note and the second will. He certainly had a motive for doing so. But how could he have duplicated his father's handwriting so perfectly as to convince ten people, one of whom was a professional handwriting expert, that the will was undoubtedly in his father's hand? Moreover, Marshall's widow readily admitted that it was the handwriting of her father-in-law, even though she stood to lose a great deal of property by doing so. So the hoax explanation seems quite implausible.

Another possible explanation is that James P. had heard about the second will, but had forgotten it, and that this subconscious "memory" finally manifested itself in the apparitional experiences. But this seems far-fetched. In view of the extent to which he would have benefited by the second will, it is very unlikely that he would have completely forgotten about it. This is contrary to what we suspect about human nature. In addition, the time between the writing of the will and the father's death was not very long—about 2½ years. Most of us have no difficulty remembering matters important to us for that length of time. When Mr. Johnson, the attorney, repeatedly questioned James P., his mother, his wife, and his daughter about whether any of them could have had normal subconscious knowledge of the note or the second will, they claimed that such an explanation is impossible. They responded in such a way that Johnson was, as he puts it, "much impressed with the evident sincerity of these people, who had the appearance of honest, honourable country people, in well-to-do circumstances."

It must be admitted that this case has some puzzling features. If James, the father, wished to replace the first will, why didn't he reveal the existence of the second? Why did he hide it, along with a note revealing its location? This is strange behavior, but then he had a reputation for being very eccentric. And it may be that he meant to reveal it, but procrastinated until he no longer had the opportunity to do so. It must be remembered that he died suddenly from a fall.

There is one other possible explanation which should

not be ignored. It is that the subliminal portion of the mind of James P. could have received the information about the will clairvoyantly, or else telepathically from the mind of James, the father, when he was still living. And then the information was passed on to consciousness in the form of an apparition. This possibility cannot be completely ruled out. But it involves a remarkable incidence of paranormal activity and thus may make as great a demand on our credulity as the claim that James Chaffin, Sr. survived death.

In addition to cases of this sort in which a single percipient views the apparition, there are well-attested cases in which two or more people simultaneously view the same apparition. Two or more people present together in the same room or area may see, for example, a figure which seems to enter through a closed door, move across the room, and disappear into the opposite wall. On comparing their observations, they may find that each saw different parts of the same figure, just as each would have seen from his own position if a living person had crossed the room.

Such "collective" experiences are often characteristic of another type of apparition called a ghost or a haunting. A ghost is an apparition which recurs and seems to be connected with a particular place rather than intended for a particular witness. One of the most remarkable and best authenticated cases is that of the Morton Ghost. It was described by Miss R.C. Morton (a pseudonym) who at the time was preparing to become a physician and who was apparently not fearful of the apparition but viewed it with only scientific curiosity.

Miss Morton states that having gone up to her room one night she heard someone at the door. Upon opening it she saw the figure of a tall lady dressed in black, standing at the head of the stairs. As the figure began to descend the stairs, Miss Morton followed, curious as to what it might be. However, the piece of candle she was carrying went out, and so she went back to her room. She says,

> The figure was that of a tall lady, dressed in black of a soft woollen material, judging from the slight sound in moving. The face was hidden in a handkerchief held in the right hand. This is all I noticed then; but on further occasions, when I was able to observe her more closely, I saw the upper part of the left side of the forehead, and a little of the hair above. Her left hand was nearly hidden by her sleeve and a fold of her dress. As she held it down a portion of the widow's cuff was visible on both wrists, so that the whole impression was that of a lady in widow's weeds.[6]

During the next two years Miss Morton saw the figure about half-a-dozen times. It was also seen by one of her sisters, by the housemaid, and by her brother and another boy. Miss Morton made a practice of following the apparition down the stairs into the drawing room. She tried to touch the apparition, but it always eluded her. When she tried to corner it, it would simply disappear. She spoke to it but never received any reply. Describing the first time she spoke to it, she says,

> I opened the drawing room door softly and went in, standing just by it. She came in past me and walked to the sofa and stood still there, so I went up to her and asked her if I could help her. She moved, and I thought she was going to speak, but she only gave a slight gasp and moved towards the door. Just by the door I spoke to her again, but she seemed as if she were quite unable to speak. She walked into the hall, then by the side door she seemed to disappear as before.[7]

Miss Morton tried to photograph the apparition but was unsuccessful. She stretched a number of fine strings across the stairway where it was accustomed to walk, but it passed right through them without breaking them. She mentions that its footsteps were audible and characteristic. They were heard not only by Miss Morton, but by her three sisters and by the cook.

The apparition continued to appear for a period of seven years. To begin with it appeared so solid and lifelike that it was often mistaken for a real person. It gradually became less distinct, but at all times was such that light would not pass through it. It was seen in the orchard and the garden as well as in the house. It was seen in the house by several people. However, Miss Morton's father could not see it even when its location was pointed out to him. In all, it was seen and/or heard by about twenty people, many of whom had not previously heard of the apparition or of the sounds. It was described in the same way by all of them. The visual description of it corresponded to a woman who had lived in the house some time before her death and whose life there had been unhappy.

Another point of interest in connection with this case is Miss Morton's apparent telepathic communication with her friend, Miss Catherine Campbell, on the night she first saw the apparition. Miss Campbell writes,

> On the night on which Miss Morton first spoke to the figure, as stated in her account, I myself saw her telepathically. I was in my room (I was then residing in the North of England, quite one hundred miles away from Miss Morton's home), preparing for bed, between twelve and half-past, when I seemed suddenly to be standing close by the door of the housemaid's cupboard [in the Morton house], so facing the short flight of stairs leading to the top landing. Coming down these stairs, I saw the figure, exactly as described, and about two steps behind Miss Morton herself, with a dressing-gown thrown loosely around her, and carrying a candle in her hand. . . . The black dress, dark head-gear, widow's cuffs and handkerchief were plainly visi-

ble, though the details of them were not given me
by Miss Morton till afterwards, when I asked her
whether she had not seen the apparition on that
night.[8]

The next day Miss Campbell wrote to Miss Morton, describing the apparition and asking her if she had seen it
that night, without knowing that the latter *had* in fact
done so until sometime later. Miss Campbell added that
this was the only vision she had ever had.

We are not in a position to dismiss hauntings as mere
superstition of primitive people or mythology of ancient
cultures. For they are apparently occurring at the present
time. Dr. Thelma Moss, for example, tells of a ghost that
is apparently still in residence in England.[9] In 1964 an
NBC television crew was filming some of the famous
haunted houses of England when they apparently got into
trouble with a ghost. The crew was headed by Philip de
Felitta, an experienced film director, who had gone to England with thorough-going skepticism, expecting to provide the American public with an interesting view of
some of England's exquisite old homes and nothing more.
And nothing strange did occur until they arrived at Long-
leat Manor, which was allegedly haunted by the Green
Lady Ghost. Bizarre things began to happen as soon as
the crew set up their equipment. The telephone went
dead, lights blew up, time-lapse cameras were turned off,
and a piece of their heavy equipment inexplicably broke
loose from its anchor and crashed over the spiral stair-
case to the floor below. But the most uncanny thing was
that they couldn't get any pictures. Their film developed
into a greenish-yellow haze unlike anything they had ever
seen before. They tried different cameras and new film,
which was guaranteed to be in mint condition, but nothing helped.

The delays were costing NBC a lot of money, and de
Fellita was becoming so desperate that he decided to take

the advice of their psychic consultant and ask the ghost
for permission to film the Manor. He was advised to go
to the focal area of activity (viz., the third-floor library)
in total darkness at midnight and to speak respectfully.
When later asked how he felt about what he was doing,
he said,

> You know, I was scared. But more than scared, I
> felt so damn foolish! All this was happening, and I
> couldn't deny it was happening, but still, some part
> of me couldn't accept it. You get brainwashed into
> believing there's no such animal as a ghost. Ghosts
> are for Halloween, for horror movies. But for
> Christ's sake, they can't screw up a TV show! But
> there I was, walking into an empty library at mid-
> night to have a talk with some ghosts. And believe
> me, I talked seriously and respectfully.[10]

De Felitta didn't receive any answer from the ghost,
but he had the feeling that everything was going to be
fine. And he was right. The time-lapse camera near the
library had worked all night and the film that they ran
the next day came out beautifully! As a special bonus,
the infrared film of the camera near the library revealed
what looked like a blob of light emerging from a doorway down the hall, floating toward the camera, and then
disappearing through a door near the camera. It appeared
just after de Felitta spoke his piece in the library.

Contrary to popular belief, "haunted" houses are not
always old and abandoned. Many are modern, comfort-
able homes inhabited by several members of a family,
most of whom have encountered the ghost. A woman
from Los Angeles provides a very interesting account of
her "haunted" house:

> In September 1971, my husband and I purchased
> the house we are presently living in. The house is
> six years old, a trilevel, with the master bedroom

located up a short flight of stairs (5) and three bed-
rooms and bath up a flight of 10 stairs.

My husband and I sleep with the bedroom door
open so we can listen for our little boy, C— (3½).
One night something woke me (I don't know what;
as far as I can remember I hadn't been dreaming).
I saw a red light, which seemed to be about 5 or
more feet in height and 3 or more feet in width,
moving slowly up the stairs. I became frightened
and woke my husband. But when he woke, the light
was gone.

The next few weeks went by normally, except for
some incidents involving C—. Several times he
would look up from what he was doing and say,
"What, daddy? What, daddy?" as if his father was
calling him, when in actuality his father was not
home. I mentioned these incidents to my husband
but we attached little importance to them.

It was toward the end of November when I noticed
a drastic change in my feelings about the house.
Before I had found it a lovely home, but my feelings went from liking to hatred. I became depressed and unhappy, which is not like me at all.
Trying to trace the source brought me back to the
house. Although my rational instincts told me that
was ridiculous, my survival instincts told me it was
true. January 4 we put our house up for sale.

During this time we would occasionally hear strange
noises, nothing frightening, but when C— would
hear them, he would say, "What's that?" and we
would tell him, "That's just the furnace." So after
that whenever he heard any strange noise he would
say, "That's the furnace."

The disturbing thing happened one Saturday, while
we were watching a TV show called the Sixth
Sense. It was an episode of a man who was drowned
coming back to haunt his wife. He is dripping wet,

but there is an unearthly quality about him. When C— saw this apparition he exclaimed, "There's Furnace." Just after he says this, the wife on TV sees her husband and screams. C— says, "Furnace make lady scream." He was not in the least upset by seeing the apparition.

But perhaps the strangest thing of all is that my feelings about the house changed abruptly in mid-February. One morning I woke and felt my normal self, eager to start a new day. And I have felt that way ever since. This change of feeling occurred approximately at the time C— said, "Furnace went out the door."[11]

When we attempt to understand what is happening in cases such as these and try to assess the weight they have as evidence for survival, we must keep in mind that there are several good cases on record of apparitions of the living. In such cases, the person whose apparition appears to another is often in a crisis situation under severe physical and/or emotional distress. These apparitional experiences can be veridical in the way that apparitions of the dead can be—by revealing accurate information which, it would seem, could not have been acquired in any normal fashion. Sometimes the person who appears to another in an apparition was thinking of the latter and desires to communicate a message or to be with him, but this is often not the case.

Because apparitions of the living are so similar to apparitions of the dead, they are often regarded as decreasing the weight of apparitions as evidence for survival. But we need not regard them as doing that. For they can be explained in terms of a theory which construes apparitions of the dead (or some of them) as being just what they seem to be—manifestations of the continued existence of a person after death. This theory is the telepathic theory of apparitions. It incorporates some fairly well-established features of telepathy. It is pretty clear that telepathy is a two-stage process. In the first stage, the telepathic impression affects some level of the recipient's subliminal mind. In the second stage, this impression manifests itself in consciousness. This manifestation may take various forms, but the most dramatic is when the impression is manifested in the form of a detailed, vivid, and very lifelike reproduction of the person from whom the impression comes. It may be so lifelike that the percipient is convinced at first that the person is physically present before his eyes. But, in reality, he is experiencing a telepathically-induced hallucination.

On this view, then, apparitions of the living and of the dead can be understood in the same way. In the case of the former, the telepathic agent (the person from whom the telepathic impression comes) is still living, whereas in the case of the latter it is a deceased person who has survived death. Though the deceased person lacks a physical body, he remembers what he looked like when alive. This memory image is telepathically conveyed to the percipient and eventually gets manifested in the percipient's consciousness in the form of a hallucinatory figure which resembles the deceased person as he looked when alive.

A strong point for this view is the ease with which it can be used to explain a fact which is very puzzling in other views—the fact that apparitions almost always appear as wearing clothing. At first glance, the fact that apparitions are clothed may not seem surprising, but a little reflection will reveal that this fact is a mind-dependent entity. If, for example, an apparition is a quasi-physical double of the person's physical body (as astral body theorists and others suggest) which, like the physical body, has objective, mind-independent existence, then how can we account for the fact that it is clothed? What could the clothing be? As someone wittily put this difficulty, "If ghosts have clothes, then clothes have ghosts."

Obviously, the clothing cannot be real physical clothing. Presumably, it would have to be of the same "stuff" as the double, with the same causal properties. If the double passes right through physical obstacles without hindrance, so do the clothes it is wearing. When it suddenly disappears, they do also. Thus even though it is tempting to try to explain away the clothes as vivid, perceptual-like memory images of the deceased's clothing, consistency dictates otherwise. But the consequences of being consistent and conceding that the clothes are quasi-physical like the double of the physical body are equally unsatisfying. For if clothes have quasi-physical doubles, then there is nothing to prevent one from concluding that everything and sundry has a double. But this seems ridiculous. Such a gratuitous doubling of the various inhabitants of the world does not seem to be worth taking seriously.

The telepathic theory of apparitions, on the other hand, provides a very plausible account of the clothing. The clothing is telepathically induced into the experiential field of the percipient just as are the other features of the apparition. The telepathic agent, if living, thinks of himself as clothed in a certain way and of being in a particular situation. If deceased, he remembers what he looked like, and these memories would include the clothes he wore. As I have suggested in detail earlier, he may have an image body which appears to him to be very much like his former physical body because it is based on memories of his former body which now have the lifelikeness and the forcefulness of perception. And this image body would appear to him to be clothed since it is based on memory images (primarily visual and tactual) of his physical body which was ordinarily clothed.

In this view, then, an apparition of a person occurs when his image body appears in the experiential field of another. According to the telepathic theory, telepathy is the process by which this takes place whether the apparition is of the living or of the dead. By looking at the role of the image body, we can observe a basis for relating apparitions, OBEs, and dreams. We can view all three as manifestations of the same basic phenomenon. In an OBE, a person generates an image body which, like the body that he sometimes dreams that he has, becomes the one from which he temporarily does his perceiving and feels himself to be "in," but which is ordinarily not perceived by any other person (or, at any rate, not by any other embodied person). In an apparition, however, one's image body appears to another, but is ordinarily not the center of one's perceptual experiences. Indeed, the one whose image body it is may not even know that the apparition is being experienced. Of course, this may not be the case if the person whose image body it is is discarnate. More briefly, then, one's image body appears to oneself (if it appears at all) in the OBE and the dream, but in the apparition it appears to another.

Though an apparition of the dead can be understood by supposing that the image body of the discarnate person somehow makes its way, perhaps by means of telepathy, into the perceptual experience of a living person, it need not be supposed that the discarnate person is consciously or voluntarily sending a telepathic message. By supposing that the discarnate person is sometimes not conscious of what is happening, the difference between hauntings and those apparitions in which the deceased seems to be trying to communicate with the living becomes readily understandable. The apparition of James Chaffin, Sr., for example, certainly appeared to be trying to communicate, something which the deceased, if they have thoughts and emotions, might be expected to do. But haunting apparitions, on the other hand, may seem puzzling because they usually behave in a semiautomatic, dreamy manner, going through a certain routine time and again whenever they appear. They do not display any signs of consciousness. But this is not surprising if the discarnate person who is the source of such an apparition is not trying to communicate and is not even conscious of the effect that he is producing. Instead of being produced by conscious intention or voluntary activity on his part, the source of a haunting apparition may be some kind of brooding memory that he has of an experience that he had when alive. He may be only dimly aware of it, attending to it with a minimum of consciousness, much as someone might absentmindedly and mechanically go through a routine without consciously attending to it.

11

MENTAL MEDIUMSHIP

PERHAPS THE MOST IMPRESSIVE EMPIRICAL EVIDENCE FOR survival is that provided by certain cases in which the deceased seem to be communicating with us through persons known as mediums or automatists. A medium or automatist is a person, usually a woman, who, according to the survival view, acts as a transmitter between our world and the world of those who have died. The medium usually goes into a trance state prior to such communications and then begins to give out statements automatically, that is, not consciously or intentionally as in ordinary speech or writing. Thus such persons are appropriately referred to as automatists. These statements may be written automatically by the hand of the automatist while she is in trance or while her attention is differently engaged. Or they may be spoken by the vocal organs of the entranced automatists. But whatever the means by which they are expressed, the appearances suggest that the intelligence and the will of the medium are not involved in the production of them. It is as though a different person is temporarily using the body of the medium to express himself. For, at least in the best cases, the voice, the handwriting, the verbal mannerisms, the ways in which ideas are associated, and the fund of information exhibited are notably different from those of the medium in her normal state. Even more remarkably, they are often characteristic of and claimed to emanate from a deceased friend or relative of someone who is sitting with the medium at the time (i.e., the sitter). In some cases the information revealed is thoroughly astounding in that it would seem to be knowledge which could be possessed only by the deceased person whom the communicating personality claims to be.

These communications which purport to come to us from the dead can be divided roughly into three kinds. First, there are those which purport to give us evidence for the continuing existence of persons after death. Secondly, there are those which allegedly explain the methods and processes used in communicating with the living through mediums. And, thirdly, there are those which claim to be descriptions of that other world in which deceased persons continue to live.

CONTROLS AND COMMUNICATORS

When the medium goes into trance she is usually taken over by a personality who claims to be a "controlling spirit" or "control," for short. The control, who claims to be a discarnate person more expert than others at the difficult task of manipulating the body and speech organs of a medium, regularly appears at the various sittings when the medium goes into trance. It has the same voice, vocabulary, and mannerisms each time it appears. It often displays a very accurate memory of what transpired during previous sittings when it was in control and shows as much evidence of being one and the same person, in spite of gaps when it is not in control of the medium's body, as does the medium's normal personality.

The control must be distinguished from other personalities who also claim to be surviving spirits of deceased persons and who wish to communicate with the sitters. These communicators, as they are called, usually appear to be giving their messages to the control who then passes them on to the sitters. The function of the control in such a situation might be compared to a telephone operator during a long-distance call with a poor connection as she relays the messages back and forth between the two parties. Sometimes, however, the control appears to give way to one of the communicators and then a new voice, manner, and personality issue forth from the body of the medium. This new voice is quite different from either that of the normal personality of the medium or of her control. It claims to come from one or another of the sitter's dead friends or relatives who was previously communicating only indirectly through the control. And sometimes this new personality appears to the sitters to have characteristics and mannerisms just like those of the deceased person it claims to be.

It should be noted that the normal personality of the medium is usually ignorant of what has been happening during the time that the control or the communicators were employing her body, just as someone who has been talking in his sleep is ignorant of what he has been doing or saying, and rapidly forgets what he had been dreaming. The control, on the other hand, frequently claims to be aware of all that the medium had been doing, perceiving, or thinking when the normal personality was in control of the body. And when these claims can be and have been tested, they have usually turned out to be true.

Before examining some cases of mediumship in detail it may be helpful to take a brief look at the various possible ways of explaining these remarkable phenomena.

Bearing them in mind as we examine the data will help in our evaluation of it. There seems to be only three possible explanations, one normal, and the other two, paranormal. The normal explanation is that the medium acquires information about the sitters and their deceased relatives before the sitting (or séance) in a perfectly normal way and then during the seance fraudulently construes it as communication emanating from the dead. Either the medium consciously and willfully gathers the information prior to the séance or she picks it up normally, but unintentionally, as by scanning books and newspapers, and then unwittingly utilizes it during the séance. But, in either case, the communications are to be explained in terms of fraud and deception, of either a conscious or unconscious sort. One of the paranormal explanations is that the medium (or her trance personality) acquires the information in question by means of extrasensory perception. More specifically, the trance personality acquires it either telepathically from the minds of the living, or by clairvoyantly apprehending existing facts and records, or through a retrocognitive apprehension of past events, or by a combination of these. The other paranormal explanation is the survival hypothesis—the view that these communications (or some of them) are just what they purport to be, i.e., messages from deceased persons who have survived death. Of course, defenders of the survival view as well as defenders of the ESP hypothesis readily admit that the great majority of mediumship phenomena can be explained away as due to fraud, trickery, and deception. For this is an area which has been exploited a great deal by frauds and imposters. But, they would argue, not all can be so explained.

MRS. PIPER'S MEDIUMSHIP

As might be expected, mediums differ greatly in personal characteristics and degree of talent. Great mediums are very rare, probably rarer than great artists. Mrs. Leonore Piper, an American medium, was one of the greatest. She was the most impressive medium studied by the early members of the Society for Psychical Research (S.P.R.). She was under expert observation for twenty-five years. It appears that she was studied by more men of science, more systematically and minutely, and for more years than any other medium. William James, the famous American philosopher, was the first of these to study her. Then Dr. Richard Hodgson, the secretary of the S.P.R., began an intensive study of her. This very competent and highly critical investigator continued his investigation of Mrs. Piper for eighteen years. Both James and Hodgson were first exposed to Mrs. Piper at a time when they were very skeptical of all mediums and suspected fraud and trickery of all of them. Hodgson took elaborate precautions to ensure against any possibility of fraud. He had both Mrs. Piper and her husband under surveillance by detectives for several weeks to see if they were attempting to gather information about the friends and relatives of the sitters. But nothing even remotely suspicious was ever found. As an extra precaution, Hodgson made a practice of introducing sitters under false names, allowed them to enter the room only after Mrs. Piper had gone into trance, and then seated them behind her where she would have been unable to see them even if her eyes had been open.

James and Hodgson were so impressed with Mrs. Piper that they advised the S.P.R. to invite her to London where she could be studied under conditions which would guarantee her ignorance of the people who would sit with her. There she was studied by Sir Oliver Lodge, Henry Sidgwick, F.W.H. Myers, and other distinguished investigators. They, too, were cautious, skeptical investigators who gave her no chance to acquire information about the people who would be present when she was in trance. Lodge met her when she arrived and took her directly to his own home where elaborate precautions were taken to make sure that she was not cheating. Among other things her luggage was searched, the few letters she received were examined, and the sitters were introduced under false names. Yet she continued to come up with astounding information, much of which was about the deceased friends and relatives of the sitters, and which, it would seem, could not have been acquired by her in any normal manner.

The communications received by Professor James Hyslop[1] are a good example of such information provided by Mrs. Piper. Hyslop, a member of the S.P.R., was one of the many people to have sittings with Mrs. Piper during the period when her mediumship was being closely observed by Richard Hodgson. The communications received by Hyslop purported to come from several of his dead relatives, but primarily from his deceased father. Those allegedly from his father refer to several conversations that Hyslop had with his father and to many special facts and incidents in the father's life. They include such matters as the fact that the father had a mark near his left ear, that he had trouble with his left eye, that he had a horse named Tom, that he used to have one square bottle and one round bottle on his desk, that at one time he wore a black skull cap at night, that he used to carry a brown-handled knife which he used to trim his nails, etc. Some of these matters were unknown to Professor Hyslop, but after inquiring about them they were found to be true. The communications also contained various familiar expressions and pieces of advice which the father had been in the habit of uttering, and they were worded in ways characteristic of him.

Though many of these facts are very trivial, this does

not detract from their significance. Indeed, their triviality increases their significance. For trivial facts are not likely to become matters of public knowledge and thus would be very difficult for the medium to acquire in any normal fashion. They are the sort of facts which we would ordinarily find to be particularly convincing in establishing the identity of someone we knew well and with whom we have shared various experiences. Suppose, for example, that I receive a telephone call from a person claiming to be my brother who lives in another part of the country, and that the connection is very bad so that the operator, who seems to be rather obtuse and incoherent, has to relay the messages back and forth. Because of these circumstances I am in doubt about whether the person I am communicating with is really my brother. If this is the case, then his referring to trivial and intimate matters, some of which are known only to the two of us, is precisely the sort of evidence that I would find convincing in establishing his identity. Communications of trivial matters of this sort, purporting to come from dead relatives, were given out by Mrs. Piper to dozens and dozens of sitters over the years.

Can we account for such communications if we do not suppose that they are just what they purport to be—messages from the deceased? As we have seen, the fraud hypothesis seems to be totally untenable in the case of Mrs. Piper. The very competent and cautious investigators who examined her vouched for her honesty. William James, for example, writes, "I should be willing now to stake as much money on Mrs. Piper's honesty as on that of anyone I know, and am quite satisfied to leave my reputation for wisdom or folly, so far as human nature is concerned, to stand or fall by this declaration."[2] However, the ESP explanation is one that we must carefully consider. It may be that the trance personality of Mrs. Piper acquires her information about the lives and personal characteristics of the deceased by means of ESP and then imitates the manner of the deceased person whom it represents as the source of the information. Perhaps the trance state is a form of self-induced hypnosis which, like other hypnotic states, is one in which the subject often displays a remarkable capacity to imitate other persons. Furthermore, this trance state may be similar to the dream state in being conducive to the exercise of otherwise latent ESP capacities. Because of this feature of the dream state, and, quite possibly of other trance states, much present research on ESP is conducted on people who are asleep and dreaming. Such matters render the ESP hypothesis more plausible.

The ESP hypothesis gains strong support from the fact that some cases of communications which purport to come from the deceased could not have had such a source; for the persons from whom they are claimed to come are either fictitious or are still living at the time. A good example of the latter is a communication received by the psychical researcher, Dr. S.G. Soal,[3] through a medium he was testing. Mrs. Blanche Cooper, the medium, produced for him a communication purporting to come from a Gordon Davis, one of Soal's boyhood friends who Soal believed to have been killed in the First World War. The Gordon Davis personality appeared to "control" the speech organs of the medium and spoke in the manner characteristic of Gordon Davis. The personality apparently believed itself to be the deceased Gordon Davis and spoke of experiences that Davis and Soal had shared. It then went on to describe in considerable detail a house Davis had once lived in. The description included the view from the house, various pictures in it, a black china bird on the piano, and other matters. However, about eighteen months later, Soal was surprised to discover that Gordon Davis was very much alive and employed as a real estate agent. A professional diary that Davis kept revealed that at the time of the sitting, Davis was interviewing a client and completely unaware of his apparent presence many miles away. Equally surprising is the fact that Soal found Davis living in the house that the Davis personality had described, even though he had not moved to that house until some time *after* Soal's sitting with the medium!

Apparently, the medium (or her trance personality) acquired the information about Davis and the belief that he was dead telepathically from the mind of S.G. Soal. The information about the house suggests some sort of precognition since neither Soal nor Davis possessed that information at the time of the sitting. Rosalyn Heywood, a contemporary psychical researcher, describes her personal experience of a case in which the medium was quite obviously acquiring her information from the mind of the sitter. She writes:

> Soon after the Second World War I decided to test a medium by having an anonymous sitting with her and mentally asking the fate of a German-friend, of whom I heard nothing since 1938. He was a prominent man of great integrity, and I feared he must have been killed, either by the Nazis or the Russians. He soon appeared to turn up at the sitting, gave his Christian name, spoke through the medium in character and reminded me of various pleasant experiences which he had shared with my family in America, and I had forgotten. He then said he had been killed in grim circumstances which he did not want to talk about. After the sitting I made enquiries as to his fate. He was eventually traced by the Swiss Foreign Office to a neutral country, and in reply to a letter from me he said that he had escaped both Nazis and Russians, had married, was living in two rooms and had never been so happy in his life. Here, then, it looks as if the medium, unknown to herself, was building a picture of the German from my subconscious memories and my fears as to his fate.[4]

The communications received through Mrs. Piper were not entirely free of this phenomenon. G. Stanley Hall once received through Mrs. Piper communications from a young woman, Bessie Beals, who was a totally fictitious person conceived by him for the purpose of testing the medium. Thus it is quite obvious that at least some of the Piper communications which purport to come from the deceased are really not at all what they seem to be, but are due to the ESP capacity and dramatizing powers of the medium's trance personality. However, the ESP hypothesis is the hypothesis that *all* such communications which are not due to fraud and deception are explainable in terms of ESP. And so the question to which we must turn is whether any such communications cannot be so explained.

Though a hypnotized person and, presumably, the trance personality of a medium possess a remarkable capacity to dramatize and to dramatically imitate a personality, such activities must be distinguished from a dramatic interplay between different personalities in the give and take of conversation. Professor Hyslop emphasizes the great difference between the two and points out that the Piper communications contain many instances of the latter, including those purporting to come from his father. A Piper communication which illustrates this feature well came from a personality who claimed to be George Pelham (a pseudonym for Pellew), a young attorney who had died very suddenly as a result of an accident.[5] Pelham was a member of the American Society for Psychical Research and a friend of Hodgson, to whom he had mentioned that if he died first and found himself still in existence he would try very hard to communicate that fact.

This personality first appeared about four weeks after the death of George Pelham when John Hart, an old friend of Pelham's, was sitting with Mrs. Piper. The G.P. personality then began to function as Mrs. Piper's control and was thoroughly tested in the sittings that followed. Many of George Pelham's friends attended these sittings and the G.P. personality was asked to identify them. Out of over 150 people who attended these sittings, G.P. picked out 30 of Pelham's friends without making a single mistake. He spoke to them of experiences they had shared with him and responded in the "give and take" of conversation as George Pelham would have done. As Hodgson puts it, in each case "the recognition was clear and full, and accompanied by an appreciation of the relations which subsisted between G.P. living and the sitters."[6] G.P.'s spontaneity and his faithfulness to the thought and manner of George Pelham was very convincing. Even the cautious and critical Hodgson seems to be convinced as he writes,

> The continual manifestation of this personality . . . with its own reservoir of memories, with its swift appreciation of any reference to friends of G.P., with its 'give and take' in little incidental conversations with myself, has helped largely in producing a conviction of the actual presence of the G.P. personality which it would be quite impossible to impart by any mere enumeration of verifiable statements.[7]

To account for this interplay between different personalities on the ESP hypothesis, we would have to suppose not only that the medium's trance personality has the very remarkable capacity to almost instantaneously acquire, by means of ESP, information about matters known to George Pelham as it is needed in the conversation, but to translate instantly the items so acquired into the form of a dramatic and highly authentic impersonation of Pelham as he would have acted in the give and take of lively conversation with someone who had shared various experiences with him. When we converse with a friend with whom we have shared experiences, we find that we can refer indirectly to some intimate matter and our friend immediately understands what we are talking about and responds appropriately. If he is a sensitive person we notice that his emotional attitude shifts appropriately from, say, one of levity and merriment to one of seriousness as he senses such a change in our own. Such conversational understanding was characteristic of the G.P. personality. And it apparently had much to do with Hodgson's eventual acceptance of the survival hypothesis. As he concludes Section 6 of his report he says,

> I cannot profess to have any doubt but that the chief "communicators," to whom I have referred in the foregoing pages, are veritably the personalities that they claim to be, that they have survived the change we call death, and that they have directly communicated with us whom we call living, through Mrs. Piper's entranced organism.[8]

However, before deciding whether or not to agree with him let us examine the cases of two other great mediums.

Mrs. Leonard's Mediumship

Mrs. Osborne Leonard was a trance medium who was studied by members of the S.P.R. for over forty years. Like Mrs. Piper, her honesty was above question. During these many years, no detective or anyone else ever found the slightest basis for suspicion. Her mediumship is important not only because it provides evidence that some people have survived death, but also because it allegedly provides information about the conditions of life after death and the processes used in communicating with the living by way of a medium.

Mrs. Leonard had a single regular control and a number of communicators associated with various sitters. Her regular control called herself "Feda" and claimed to be the surviving spirit of an ancestress of Mrs. Leonard. One of the most important series of sittings was those with Rev. C. Drayton Thomas.[9] In these sittings the primary communicators claimed to be his father, John, and his sister, Etta. Mrs. Leonard had never met nor even heard of the persons whom these communicators claimed to be before the sittings began. The sittings continued for many years, and Thomas kept elaborate records of all that was said or done during them.

Sometimes the John and Etta personalities would communicate indirectly through Feda, and other times it would seem that one or the other would take possession of the medium's body and use it to communicate directly with the sitter. These two personalities provided detailed explanations of the processes involved in each method of communication.

Direct communication involving the apparent possession of the medium's body by the communicator would come about in the following way: During a sitting in which Feda has been in control and acting as intermediary between communicator and sitter, she will announce that she is about to give way to that communicator. For a moment, nothing happens. Then, after a long exhalation of breath, the medium's body goes limp and lies as in a faint unless supported. Now a new voice issues from the medium's lips which, the sitters contend, is often remarkably like that of the deceased person whom the communicator claims to be. The appearances are that a deceased person (viz., John or Etta Thomas) is using the speech organs of the medium to communicate.

These first attempts at possession by a communicator are usually attended with great difficulties. The voice is very feeble at first, and the medium's body remains limp. The duration of the possession is very short. But gradually, as though the communicator is learning how to control the medium's body, the voice becomes as strong as Feda's or the normal Mrs. Leonard's, and the medium's body is able to sit in an upright position again without support. At this stage the communicator may be able to talk for an hour or more.

Normally Mrs. Leonard is not aware of what transpires when a communicator is in control of her body, just as she is not when Feda is in control. Moreover, Feda seems to be equally ignorant of what takes place. However, both Feda and the communicators claim to be individuals who have lives independently of Mrs. Leonard's body and that they meet and communicate with each other in that independent state.

The communicators claim that taking possession of the medium's body is a difficult feat to accomplish, and that even when they are highly successful, communication is difficult because they are not very clear-minded when in possession and tend to forget things that they would otherwise have no problem remembering. Their explanation of why this occurs is most interesting. They claim that the ordinary division of mind into conscious and subconscious layers disappears at death, but recurs during possession with the conscious portion of their mind becoming the portion in control of the medium's body. They often tend to forget altogether that other portion of their mind which would correspond with our subconscious. And even when that does not happen, it is harder for them to gain access to its contents than it is for us to get in touch with the contents of our subconscious. This situation, they say, is due to the fact that, when in possession, what is then the conscious portion of their mind is diminished by their having to share the medium's brain and nervous system with the medium's mind. Consequently, the conscious portion of their mind when in possession is smaller in relation to their subconscious than is the case with us.

Whatever we make of this account, we must admit that

it would help to explain in a way that is consistent with the survival hypothesis the fact that so many communications claiming to come from deceased persons who were very intelligent and knowledgeable while alive contain much that is confused, incoherent, inaccurate, irrelevant, and trivial. If the process of communication inevitably involves such difficulties, then these shortcomings are what we might have expected.

It is interesting to note that the John and Etta personalities claim to have bodies with sense organs. Etta makes a distinction between perceiving through the medium's sense organs (when in possession of the medium's body) and perceiving through her own. She claims that when in possession of the medium's body, she hears what the sitter says through the medium's ears, but generally does not see anything by way of the medium's eyes. And she claims that she uses her own sense organs to see or hear one of the other communicators. However, she says that she avoids using her own sense organs when in possession of the medium's body since doing so tends to cause her to lose control of it.

Many of the communications were received by C. Drayton Thomas via a process of indirect communication. Feda would act as an intermediary between the communicator and sitter, receiving messages from the communicator and then passing them on to the sitter in her own voice and manner via the speech organs of the medium. The communicators, John and Etta, had numerous comments to make on the nature of this process also. In this process, too, they claim, they must grapple with confusion and inability to remember. They speak of an emanation or "power" which issues primarily from the medium. It extends for some distance around the medium and is necessary for communication to take place. John and Etta claim that in order to communicate with Feda they must enter the "region" of the emanation which they can feel but usually cannot see. But once they do so, they immediately begin to feel mentally unclear and fail to recall things that they could easily remember at other times. In the words of C. Drayton Thomas, ''My father has repeatedly mentioned that his mind is not so clear after entering the circle of power, yet only when within it can he transmit thought in words.''[10] And Etta said:

> It is a no-man's land between the two conditions, yours and ours. . . . It is supposed that communication concerns earth people and spirit people, whereas there is also the peculiar *bridgeway* which has to be used and which is neither one nor the other, but has some of the characteristics of each.[11]

Sometimes they must temporarily withdraw to reorganize their thought or recall a memory and then reenter to continue the communication.

The communicators distinguish two different ways in which they can give messages to Feda. They can actually speak to her, or they can use one of several modes of telepathy. As Prof. C.D. Broad points out in an excellent study of Mrs. Leonard's mediumship,[12] they distinguish five different modes of telepathic communication. Suppose they wished to convey a message about a horse. They could actually speak to her (i.e., generate in her an auditory sensation); or they could generate telepathically in her mind (1) an auditory image of the word ''horse'' (i.e., as one hears a spoken word or melody in one's mind), or (2) a visual image of the written word ''horse,'' or (3) a visual image of such an animal, or (4) a symbolic visual image such as an image of a jockey with a whip, or (5) the thought of a horse without images or symbols. If they can actually speak to her, one might wonder why they use telepathy, but they say that it is easier for them to induce a telepathically generated image or thought in her mind than it is to generate actual sensations of sound.

In addition to these modes of telepathy, the John personality also distinguishes between two processes which can be considered telepathic. On the one hand, there is the deliberate projection by the communicator of an image or thought into Feda's mind. On the other, there is the reading of the communicator's mind by Feda with the result that she becomes aware of items in his mind without his knowledge or approval of what is happening. The latter can be a source of frustration to a communicator when Feda seizes upon an irrelevant or unimportant item and then develops it in a wearisome or misleading way.

The communicators assert that Feda frequently makes mistakes about the form in which a message is conveyed to her. She sometimes says that she has been seeing or hearing a communicator when in fact they have been sending her messages telepathically. However, they agree that it is sometimes true that she does literally see or hear them. And sometimes, they say, she makes the opposite mistake of claiming to have received messages from them telepathically when the truth is that she has been literally seeing them or hearing them speak.

C. Drayton Thomas also questioned the Feda personality about the nature of her role in indirect communication. Her role is twofold: to receive the messages from the communicators and then transmit them on to the sitters. Her account of how she receives messages from the communicators complements their account. She says that the messages come to her in various forms: (1) she may hear words spoken to her, or (2) hear auditory images of them in her mind rather than auditory sensations, or (3) see visual images of the words as they appear when written, or (4) see symbolic images, or (5) apprehend the message ''in thought.'' She agrees with the communicators in distinguishing between them literally speaking and ''only mentally'' speaking to her.

Feda claims that it usually takes several sittings with a

person before she can see the communicator, although she has been hearing him speak from the first. She says that in rare cases and only with communicators she has worked with a great deal she may have an experience of simultaneous seeing, hearing, and touching the communicator. She states that she listens from within the medium's body to the sitter's voice and to the voice of the communicator. She hears both in the same literal sense, but uses two different sets of sense organs to do it—she uses the medium's ears to listen to the sitter and her own auditory sense organs to listen to the communicator, unless the latter is using telepathy to convey his message. As an additional point of interest, she notes that when the communicator is "only mentally" speaking to her (i.e., causing auditory images instead of auditory sensations to arise in her consciousness), the simultaneous occurrence of normal auditory sensations such as those produced by the sitter's voice does not confuse her. But the simultaneous presence of normal physical sounds does tend to confuse her while she is having an experience of the communicator literally talking to her. C. Drayton Thomas recorded an interesting illustration of this. Feda is relaying a message from the John personality when she has trouble hearing because of distracting sounds coming through an open window. She stops and requests that the window be closed. C. Drayton Thomas continues:

This break came in the midst of an interesting passage which flowed with ease and accuracy. I then noticed, for the first time, a sound of voices in conversation outside the room where we were sitting. Two persons were talking on the lawn outside. I asked them to speak more softly and closing the window returned to my place. Feda then said: It does not matter while your father talks mentally, but when he speaks his voice, it sounds like a real voice to Feda while in the medium.[13]

Feda's account of how she transmits messages is very confused and unclear. She speaks of trying to find the right part of the medium's brain for transmitting a certain idea. She speaks of holding an image above different parts of the medium's brain until it is drawn down and then holding it there until it becomes attached. However, she admits that these statements are not to be taken literally for the holding is done with her mind and not her hands.

The John and Etta personalities are very critical of this account. Etta says that what Feda describes in terms of holding an idea above different parts of the brain really consists in her presenting the same idea in various forms to the medium's mind until the latter finally grasps it. John says that Feda is wrong in thinking that she acts upon the medium's brain. He claims that she is really acting upon the entranced medium's *mind*, putting ideas into it telepathically, just as he and other communicators telepathically affect her own mind.

These statements that the communicators have made about the way indirect communication takes place are consistent with what the sitters observe the medium to be doing. C. Drayton Thomas observes that the medium's body is in an attitude as of listening when Feda is receiving a message. It appears to the sitter that a message is being dictated to Feda which she then repeats. As Drayton Thomas says, "Her attitude is that of one listening intently; often she bends forward as if to catch the words more distinctly, as when I ask a question and the medium bends forward in a listening attitude, Feda saying, "I'll ask him what he thinks about it.""[14]

Though many of Feda's statements and questions suggest that she has been piecing together a series of scrappy impressions which she has received telepathically, Drayton Thomas points out that in the best parts of a good sitting Feda is apparently listening to spoken words which are audible to her. As evidence of this, Thomas says, "Long passages are given a few words at a time, exactly as if they were being repeated by one listening to a dictated message.'' Moreover, Feda sometimes makes a mistake of precisely the sort which we would expect if she had misheard a word. In many cases the correct word is obvious to the sitter from the context. Thomas gives the following examples from his notes:

> Feda: Week after week for fears—(long pause as if the misheard word caused a check in the flow and a faltering). Years. Week after week for years.

> Feda: I see greatly—What did you call it? Something—I've missed something. I'm sorry. Well, he says, I see great differences.

> Feda: We cannot as—as—We cannot, What? Oh, I can't get that word. Well say it another way, Feda, he says.[15]

Perhaps the most interesting cases are those in which Feda's mistakes are corrected by what Thomas calls the "direct voice." Sometimes he (and other sitters) would hear a word or part of a sentence, or even an entire sentence, spoken in an audible whisper which appeared to come not from the medium's lips but from a point in empty space about two or three feet from her body. These utterances were usually closely related to what Feda was saying or about to say. The following are two good examples from Thomas' paper:

> Feda: Willy—What? Who's he? Willy somebody— I can't get his other name. Willy—somebody is compelling you. Wait a minute. I've mixed that up.

> D.V. (direct voice): *It is not that at all.*

> Feda: Willy-nilly? Is that right? Willy-nilly you are being compelled, etc., etc.

> Feda: Stuart thinks he will have more important

work later, though he doesn't know quite what it is.

D.V.: *At present—*

Feda: Present? He doesn't know at present. What is it, then? "NO," he said. I don't know what it is quite. "Full stop." Full stop? But at present I am helping with, etc., etc.[16]

Thomas points out how clearly the latter example indicates a distinction between speaker and listener. Feda had mistakenly joined the first two words of a new sentence to the end of a previous one. But she is pulled up short by the communicator who is finally able to indicate his meaning by saying "Full stop," and then showing Feda that the two misplaced words are to form the beginning of a new sentence.

Sometimes the mistake is quite amusing, though perhaps exasperating to communicator and control:

Feda: He says you must have good working—What? Hippopotamuses?

D.V.: *Hypotheses*.

Feda (more loudly): Hippopotamuses.

D.V.: *Hypotheses—and don't shout!*

Feda: I'm not shouting. I'm only speaking plainly.[17]

Thomas suggests that the direct voice not only enables him to check on the accuracy of Feda's relaying of the messages but provides additional evidence of a very persuasive sort that it emanates from the person whom the communicator claims to be. He writes,

Feda will speak as if she were receiving from dictation. I can often at these times catch a softly whispered sentence before hearing it repeated in the clear Feda voice. This dictation method always reaches a high degree of accuracy, and I realize that I am receiving not merely the communicator's thoughts, but also the characteristic diction.[18]

Thomas suggests that the direct voice reveals much about the speaker as it indicates annoyance, impulsiveness, urgency, humor, or other emotions and characteristics of temperament. And he states that what the direct voice revealed was often exactly in the manner of the person whom the communicator claimed to be.

Though there is much more to be studied in Mrs. Leonard's mediumship, we are now in a position to make some sort of assessment of it. When we consider the detailed, coherent series of statements and intelligent responses to questions about the conditions of life after death coming from the entranced Mrs. Leonard, it is nothing less than astonishing. As in the case of Mrs. Piper, there seems to be no normal explanation of how she could have acquired so much information about the deceased relatives of so many sitters unknown to her and then to have cast that information into the form of a dramatic, highly verisimilar impersonation of the deceased as he would have acted in the give-and-take of conversation with a friend or relative. Fraud seems to be completely ruled out, not only because she was never once observed attempting to cheat in over forty years of observation, but also because it would seem that she simply *could not* have obtained the necessary information in that way.

It is tempting to conclude that these communications are just what they are repeatedly claimed to be. The control and all of the communicators claim to be (and apparently believe themselves to be) the surviving spirits of deceased persons, and, although the communicators often disagree with the control about other matters, they are in complete agreement about this. Moreover, they managed to convince intelligent and fastidious sitters such as C. Drayton Thomas who had been in an excellent position to detect any incongruity. Their many detailed descriptions of their present experiences and of the processes used in communication with the living are consistent with one another and with the survival hypothesis. Though they claim to have bodies with sense organs which they use to communicate with one another, this is consistent with the view that their bodies are image bodies and that telepathically induced apparitions of them are involved in their communications.

As in the case of the Piper communications, the ESP hypothesis is greatly strained when we try to explain all of the Leonard trance phenomena in terms of it. Once again we observe the dramatic interplay between different personalities in conversational give-and-take—so lifelike and true to the character of the deceased that the sitters found it to be natural and convincing. Moreover, Mrs. Leonard was very successful in "proxy" sittings in which a sitter will visit the medium on behalf of another person who is not present. Success in such sittings strains the ESP hypothesis since if the sitter doesn't even know the person he is representing, then telepathy from the sitter is ruled out as the source of information.

A highly significant and well-documented proxy sitting with Mrs. Leonard was arranged by Prof. E.R. Dodds (who, incidentally, did not believe in survival).[19] He asked C. Drayton Thomas to do a proxy sitting with Mrs. Leonard. The sitting was not even at second hand, on behalf of Prof. Dobbs himself, but at third hand on behalf of a Mrs. Lewis who wanted to contact her deceased father, a Mr. Macaulay. Both Mrs. Lewis and Mr. Macaulay, who in life had been a water engineer, were completely unknown to Thomas and Mrs. Leonard. All that

Thomas was told about Mr. Macaulay was his name, his home town, and his date of death. This is probably the minimum amount of information needed to identify someone among the millions of the dead. But this bare minimum seemed to be sufficient for Feda; for she seemed to get in touch with him right away. As evidence of his identity she described his drawing room, the instruments he worked with, the mathematical formulas he used, etc., very well for someone who knew nothing of such things. She mentioned his great interest in saving water, referred to his damaged hand, gave his pet name—Puggy—for his daughter, and correctly recounted past incidents in his life. She also gave the names of some people who, she said, had shared with him an especially happy period in his life and who were now with him. Again she was correct as these people were in fact dead. One of these names puzzled her, and she said, "It might be Reece but it sounds like Riss." Finally, she added that Mr. Macaulay had proposed to his first wife on a bridge.

None of this, of course, meant anything to Thomas. He sent it to Prof. Dodds who sent it on to Mrs. Lewis. She said that all of the items given were correct, including the names. She said that her father's passion for saving water had been a family joke, and that during the happy period referred to, her schoolboy brother had hero-worshipped an older boy whose name was Rees. Her brother had stated that this boy's name was spelled "Rees," not "Reece" so often that, to tease him, his young sisters sang, "Not Reece but Riss." They became so carried away that Mr. Macaulay had to stop them.

Though these facts and incidents are trivial, this makes them more identifying of Mr. Macaulay than dramatic matters which would be more widely known or general matters which would apply to a number of people. But, more important to the question at hand, the ESP hypothesis is rendered less plausible by the communication. It seems very unlikely that Mrs. Leonard's trance personality would have telepathically tapped the mind of Mrs. Lewis, two removes away. This would be telepathy of a peculiarly roundabout sort, for which, it seems, we have no independent evidence. The studies of telepathy indicate that it usually operates between people who are emotionally linked or at least associated in some way. And the view that the trance personality can (retrocognitively) observe the past life of a deceased person seems even more unlikely. But let us look at one more medium before trying to settle this matter.

MRS. WILLET'S MEDIUMSHIP

Mrs. Willet's mediumship was quite different from that of Mrs. Piper or Mrs. Leonard and was in some respects the most interesting and impressive of the three. "Mrs. Willet" is a pseudonym. Her maiden name was Pearce-Serocold, and her married name was Mrs. Charles Coombe-Tennant. Her husband's sister was the wife of F.W.H. Myers, one of the founders of the S.P.R. and author of *Human Personality and Its Survival of Bodily Death*. After Myers' death in 1901, a personality claiming to be him figured very prominently in her mediumship. She had considerable practical ability and played a prominent role in public affairs. In 1920 she became the first woman to be appointed by the British Government as a delegate to the assembly of the League of Nations.

Mrs. Willet was not an ordinary trance medium. She had no regular control, analogous to Feda, and she was seldom, if ever, possessed by a communicator. Several phases can be distinguished in the development of her mediumship as she progressed from a stage when her state of consciousness was almost normal through hazy, dream-like states, to a condition in which her normal

consciousness had largely receded. When giving a séance, she did at times go into a state which could appropriately be called trance, but even then she did not lose
control of her body as if asleep or in a faint. There was
no appearance of her body being used by a different personality to express itself. During her periods of deeper
trance she might have an experience of seeing the communicators, or of hearing them speak, or of seeing their
facial expressions, as we see and hear in vivid dreams.
However, after resuming her normal state she remembered little or nothing of what had taken place. This unusual trance behavior is in perfect agreement with the
claims made by the personalities communicating through
her. They stated that they did not want Mrs. Willet to
become a trance medium of the usual kind who is possessed by a control or a communicator. They did not
wish to oust her mind from control of her body. Rather,
their expressed desire was that she should remain in normal control of her body and speech organs while they act
telepathically upon her mind.

The two main Willet-communicators claimed to be the
surviving spirits of Edmund Gurney, who had died in
1888, and F.W.H. Myers, who had died in 1901. Both
were classical scholars who were members of the S.P.R.
and had devoted much of their lives to the study of mediumship and other psychical phenomena. Both had
made very sizable contributions to this area. Myers'
monumental two-volume work, *Human Personality*, still
stands as a classic in its field. And Gurney, though he
died young at the height of his power, did collaborate
with Myers and Podmore in the writing of *Phantasms of
the Living*. Mrs. Willet's first communications were
claimed to come from Myers. They were in the form of
automatic writing. Her state of consciousness was almost normal, but her handwriting was not. And she was
ignorant of the meaning of what she was just about to

write, although the words themselves would come to her just before writing them.

A few months later she was told by the Myers personality to stop writing, to try to understand the ideas which were being presented, and then to record them later. She was also told then that Gurney would be involved in the experiments which were to be made with her. Sometime later she was requested by the Myers and Gurney personalities to sit in the presence of certain other people and to dictate her impressions to them. The first person who they requested as sitter was Sir Oliver Lodge, the famous physicist, who was one of the early members of the S.P.R. and had worked with Gurney on a number of projects. After many sittings with him, the Gurney personality requested that Lord Balfour come to sit with Mrs. Willet. This request was highly significant for a couple of reasons. First, Balfour had been one of Gurney's close friends, and the two had worked together in their psychical research. Balfour could be expected to be very familiar with Gurney's views about psychic phenomena. Secondly, the Gurney personality said he wanted Balfour as sitter because the latter would be interested in the processes rather than the products of communication. And, as we shall see, the Balfour sittings did deal primarily with the nature of the processes involved in communication.

The Balfour sittings when the Gurney personality was communicator provide excellent examples of the conversational give-and-take which stretches the ESP hypothesis to the breaking point. In these sittings there was no mere outpouring of views which the sitter must passively record and accept. Nor did the communicator passively accept the views of the sitter. Rather, there was constant conversational give-and-take. Balfour would go over at his leisure his notes from a sitting, making critical comments, suggestions, and noting obscure points. Then, at the next sitting, he would offer his suggestions and ask for explanations of obscure matters. The Gurney personality would try to clarify what was obscure and answer the criticisms. He would sometimes accept and sometimes emphatically reject Balfour's suggestions. A case in point involved Balfour's theory of the structure of human personality according to which different parts of an individual's mind interact telepathically with one another. The Gurney personality strongly dissented on this point, refusing to use the term "telepathy" to designate any kind of interaction between different parts of the same mind. The dramatic form of these conversations was such as to suggest that Balfour was in telephone conversation (in which Mrs. Willet's body functioned as the telephone), about psychological and philosophical topics with a very intelligent and learned friend who had traveled to a distant land where the conditions of life were strange and difficult to describe.

Like the Leonard communicators, the Myers and Gurney personalities claim that communication with the living is rendered difficult by the fact that it is not easy for them to retain their clarity of mind during this process. Their self-consciousness tends to slip away, and they find that when trying to establish contact with us they can remain aware of themselves only through the medium's awareness of them. The communication process is further hindered by the delicate balance that must be obtained between the parts of the medium's mind. The subliminal (i.e., non-conscious) portion of her mind must be attuned to their conditions if she is to receive information from them. But it must also be in touch with the supraliminal (i.e., conscious) part of her mind and thus in touch with our world, if she is to be able to express to us the information received. Such balance, they say, is difficult to obtain. Indeed, the difficulties became almost overwhelming, at least at times. Some of the communications reveal a terrible sense of struggle as when the Gurney personality, with great intensity, speaks of ". . . the passionate desire to return to drive into incarnate minds the conviction of one's own identity, the partial successes and the blank failures. . . . I know the burden of it, the burden of it to the uttermost fraction. . . ."[20]

These communicators also spoke at length of the processes involved in their communication with us through Mrs. Willet. Their account is much more sophisticated and complicated than that given by the Leonard communicators. And this is just what we ought to expect if the communicators really are who they say they are. For Myers and Gurney were scholars who were widely read in psychology and philosophy. They had studied mediumship and other paranormal phenomena in depth and had struggled to understand them. Indeed, this seems to have been the main interest in their lives. Furthermore, they were accustomed to drawing subtle distinctions and to coin new terminology in which to express them. John and Etta Thomas, on the other hand, were people of good general education, but with no special qualifications in these areas. Thus it may be that these two sets of communicators are describing essentially the same facts but from two different levels of competency.

But, as we shall see, whatever we take the Myers and Gurney personalities to be, we must admit that the Willet communications are obviously the product of an intelligent mind or minds, gifted with the capacity for drawing subtle and significant distinctions, and highly informed in the areas of philosophy, philosophical psychology, and psychical research. In particular, they show a thorough acquaintance with the ideas and terminology of Myers' book, *Human Personality and Its Survival of Bodily Death*. For the most part they are in agreement with the views presented in that book.

The Willet communicators claim that they use telepathy to affect Mrs. Willet's mind in the communication process. They carefully distinguish telepathy from other processes which might be confused with it and also distinguish different forms of telepathy. The Gurney personality has much to say about telepathy. He insists that telepathy is always a direct relationship between two minds animating *different* bodies. As mentioned earlier, he was in vigorous disagreement with Balfour about this. He distinguishes two main forms of telepathy and then subdivides the second form to yield three forms in all. He describes the first form as analogous to aiming a projectile at a target. Apparently, the communicator intentionally generates ideas, emotions, or images in the mind of the medium. One might say that he imposes his ideas, etc., on the mind of the medium. The second form is described in highly metaphorical terms which are not easy to interpret, but seem to refer to ways in which the communicator exposes the contents of his mind to the medium. As the communicator exposes his mind to the medium, two different things may happen, thus giving rise to the two subspecies of this form of telepathy. On the one hand, the communicator may deliberately select a certain idea, image, etc., for exposure which is then received by the mind of the medium. On the other hand, "a leak" may occur, in which case some content other than the one selected by the communicator may get through to the medium's mind.

The Gurney personality distinguishes all of these forms of telepathy from another process which he calls "telaesthesia." His remarks about it are obscure and somewhat inconsistent. But it seems to be comparable to the form of telepathy in which the communicator exposes certain contents of his mind to the medium. The difference is that in the expositional form of telepathy the medium's mind is passive like that of a hypnotized person, whereas in telaesthesia the medium actively and willfully reads the communicator's mind. In other words, in telaesthesia the medium's will determines what she receives from the communicator, but this is not the case in telepathic exposition. Whatever else one makes of this distinction, it is of considerable interest to note that the word "telaesthesia" was coined by Myers and defined by him in his book, *Human Personality*. Since this word was never picked up and included in the terminology of subsequent psychical researchers, it is most remarkable to observe the communicators using it in what seems to be close agreement with the way Myers originally defined it.

The communicators also distinguish the various forms of telepathy from a process called "telergy." They claim that the result of the process which they call telergy is that the medium's body is temporarily possessed by the communicator. The medium's mind is ousted from control of her body by another personality which then uses her body to express itself by writing or speech. This, they say, is the process used in the case of the usual trance medium. But, as we have seen, they insist that they wish to prevent Mrs. Willet from becoming a trance medium of the ordinary kind, such as Mrs. Leonard or Mrs. Piper. Their wish is that her mind should remain in normal control of her body while they are communicating through her by means of telepathy and telaesthesia. They repeatedly assert that they are experimenting with her, trying to develop in her a peculiar kind of mediumship. In this way, they suggest, they can better carry out their own purposes of communication with a method that will help them keep Mrs. Willet for their own use, rather than allowing her to become a medium for all and sundry.

It is certainly important to note that the word "telergy" like "telaesthesia" was coined by Myers and defined by him in *Human Personality* as the *direct* action on a person's brain and nervous system by a mind *other* than his own—an action very similar to that by way of which a person's mind normally affects his own brain and nervous system.[21] But like "telaesthesia" it never caught on. Thus the usage of such words by the communicators is certainly intriguing, especially since one of them claims to be Myers. It is also interesting to note that the communicators' extensive knowledge of Myers' book is not characterized by a mere reiteration of its contents, as one might expect in, say, hypnotically induced recall. As an illustration, in *Human Personality* Myers regards possession due to telergy as something superior to telepathic influence. But the Myers communicator speaks of telergy as "a clumsy, creaking process" inferior to telepathic control.

The communicators say that a certain preliminary process which they call "Excursus" must be completed before telepathic or telaesthetic interaction with the medium can take place. They describe this process as involving a deliberate act on the part of the medium by means of which her embodied mind frees itself to some extent from the restricting conditions of incarnate minds. Excursus is followed by a process in which communicator and medium can each select mental content from the other's mind, though part of the communicator's mind is inaccessible to the medium. At the end of the mutual selection process the medium's mind contains a mass of selected content, part of which she has acquired telaesthetically from the communicator's mind, and the remainder has been selected by the communicator. This selected content remains latent in the medium's mind until the communicator uses telepathic influence to bring it into her consciousness, whereupon she expresses it in speech or automatic writing.

PHILOSOPHICAL VIEWS

The communicators also expressed their views on certain philosophical issues. Among other things, they talk about the mind-body relation and the nature of the self. Since much of this abounds in technical philosophical terminology and subtle philosophical distinctions, it is remarkable to find it emanating from Mrs. Willet whose normal personality was neither knowledgeable of nor interested in such matters. With respect to the nature of the self, for example, the Gurney personality distinguishes three aspects: the supraliminal (i.e., the conscious self which we identify with), the subliminal, and the transcendental. The subliminal self, in turn, has three parts, all of which must be distinguished from the transcendental self.

The Gurney personality seems to be saying that it is the deepest layer of the medium's subliminal self (i.e., the one most remote from her normal consciousness) which acquires information telaesthetically from the communicator's mind and that this information must be transmitted to the most superficial layer of her subliminal self if it is to emerge in the form of words and sentences. It seems that if such transmission is to take place, the information must undergo a process of "crystallization" in the intermediate stratum. This seems to consist in converting the information which exists in the deepest layer in an unanalyzed and unverbalized form into discrete items and associating each with a symbol.

The Gurney personality claims that at death certain changes take place in the nature of the self. Some of the content of the supraliminal self is lost, but the remainder merges with the subliminal self to become the new supraliminal self. And the transcendental self becomes the new subliminal self. It is worth noting that any such changes can be expected to increase whatever difficulties there are in communicating with the living and thus help to account for the rarity of communicators worthy of the person a communicator claims to be.

APPRAISAL OF THE WILLET UTTERANCES

Now that we have examined Mrs. Willet's mediumship sufficiently to make a tentative appraisal of it, we might ask if it is at all plausible to suppose that Mrs. Willet's trance personality acquired this complicated mass of information via ESP and then translated it into a dramatic, highly verisimilar impersonation of Myers and Gurney as they would have acted in the give-and-take of conversation—an impersonation so well done that it seemed to their friend Balfour to be natural and convincing. In addition to the fact that this would require a truly remarkable abundance of ESP—much more than is independently known to occur—there are other considerations which weigh against this view. If her trance personality were creating all of this, then it would be surprising to find it bored with and bewildered by what it was doing. Yet the attitude of her trance personality (as well as that of her normal personality) can accurately be described as one of boredom and bewilderment. At one point when the Gurney personality was discussing some difficult philosophical problems in terms she did not understand, she exclaimed, "Oh, Edmund, you do *bore* me so!" And again, "you see it seems a long time since I was here with them [with Myers and his friends] and I want to talk and enjoy myself. And I've all the time, to keep on working, and seeing and listening to such boring old—Oh Ugh!"[22] At times it seemed as though her trance personality became so bored that it resisted writing or speaking about philosophical matters. When the communicators were talking about three conflicting views of the mind-body relations—interactionism, epiphenomenalism and parallelism—she had, apparently because of this resistance, great trouble communicating the comparatively simple word "interaction." At last she cried, "I've got it." And then, "Oh but now I've got to give it out. Oh, I'm all buzzing. I can't think why people talk about such stupid things. Such long stupid words."[23] When these philosophical scripts were shown to Mrs. Willet for the first time many years later, she found them incomprehensible and said that they left her utterly bored and bewildered.

Such comments and attitudes would certainly suggest that the source of the communications was independent of Mrs. Willet's own will, whether of her normal or subliminal personality. Moreover, the subject matter of the communications is certainly not of the sort which we would have expected to originate in the personality of Mrs. Willet. In the words of Prof. C.D. Broad (as he brings to a conclusion his excellent analysis of Mrs. Willet's mediumship),

> Surely it is very surprising indeed that anything of this kind should come from a lady so completely uninterested in and ignorant of philosophy as Mrs. Willet was, and that it should be couched in language and dramatic form so characteristic of the persons ostensibly communicating.[24]

THE CROSS-CORRESPONDENCES

Perhaps the mediumship phenomena which place the greatest strain on the ESP hypothesis and thereby provide the best evidence for survival are the cross-correspondences. These are correspondences between the scripts containing the communications produced by several different mediums, including Mrs. Piper and Mrs. Willet, under conditions which were such that each was ignorant of what the others were producing. Some of the mediums were widely separated and some had never met. Yet their various scripts included fragments which, though meaningless when taken alone, seemed to fall into place and become meaningful when pieced together with similar cryptic fragments from the scripts of another medium. These fragments or correspondences were in most cases concerned with recondite details of the Greek and Latin classics. Not only did they have a topic in common, but they seemed to complement one another in a manner analogous to the way in which individual pieces of a jigsaw puzzle, though individually meaningless, form a meaningful whole when correctly combined. This meaningful whole, in the view of the investigators, displayed every sign of having been *designed* by somebody with an expert knowledge of the classics.

Unfortunately, the cases of cross-correspondence are too long and elaborate to be presented in the space available here. For the scripts of the automatists involved in the cross-correspondences are hundreds of pages long. Moreover, their significance turns on references to little known items in the Greek and Latin classics, references which will not even be recognized without extensive knowledge of these classics. Yet their evidential force can be appreciated by describing in a more general way the circumstances under which they arose, the people who investigated them, their apparently meaningful framework, and the purported communicators involved.

By 1901 three distinguished Cambridge scholars, F.W.H. Myers, Edmund Gurney and Henry Sidgwick were dead. All had been founders of the S.P.R. and deeply concerned with the question of whether or not a person survives bodily death. In addition, all were keenly aware of the extreme difficulty in coming up with any evidence for survival which could not be explained by recourse to the ESP hypothesis. As we have seen, the dramatizing powers of the subconscious, along with the possibly extensive ESP capacity of the trance personality, would make it extremely difficult for the deceased, should they continue to exist, to prove their existence.

Shortly after Myers had died in 1901, Mrs. Verrall, a lecturer in classics at Cambridge and wife of the classical scholar Dr. A.W. Verrall, began to write automatic scripts which were signed "Myers." At first they were rather poorly expressed, but gradually they became more coherent and better expressed. They remained cryptic, however, as though their meaning were being concealed. About a year later, allusions to the same subjects began to appear in the scripts of the American medium Mrs. Piper, and these too claimed to come from Myers. Then, sometime later, Mrs. Verrall's daughter, Helen, began to write automatically, and it was discovered that she also had been alluding to the same subjects before she had looked at her mother's scripts. At this point, the scripts were sent to Miss Alice Johnson, secretary of the S.P.R.

Soon afterwards Mrs. Holland (pseudonym for Mrs. Fleming, a sister of Rudyard Kipling) who lived in India, and, as we might expect, had no knowledge that such strange scripts had been produced, began to produce scripts which purported to come from Myers. She was instructed in the script itself to send it to 5 Selwyn Gardens, Cambridge. She had never been to Cambridge and the address was unknown to her, but it turned out to be the address of Mrs. Verrall. She did not follow these instructions since she was very skeptical about her scripts having any external source, but she did eventually send them to Miss Johnson who dutifully filed them away without suspecting that they contained allusions to the same subjects as the Piper and Verrall scripts.

It was not until 1905 that Miss Johnson began to realize what was happening and by that time the scripts which were being produced contained the astounding claim that the discarnate Myers, Gurney, and Sidgwick had invented this scheme of giving out, through mediums isolated from one another, communications that would be unintelligible when taken individually, but which would make sense when pieced together or when a clue to their sense was supplied in a script of yet another medium. It was claimed in the scripts themselves that they had invented this scheme in order to prove their continued existence by a method that would rule out ESP from the living as an alternative explanation. When living, these men were acutely aware of how difficult it is to come up with clear-cut evidence of survival. They realized that any item which was claimed to come from a deceased person could be checked for accuracy only if there were some existing record of it or if some living person had knowledge of it. Thus it was always possible to say that the medium acquired the information by ESP from the living, or from existing records, rather than from the deceased. In view of this, it is of the greatest interest to find the script intelligences who claimed to be the discarnate Myers, Gurney, and Sidgwick saying, in effect, that they are producing evidence of a design which was not in any living mind or contained in any record. So from what could it have come if not the deceased?

The script intelligences suggest that their scheme would reduce the possibility of telepathy from the living to the vanishing point by keeping the various mediums in total ignorance of their plan. This was to be accomplished by sending fragments alluding to recondite details of the classics to various mediums isolated from one another, and then to make these fragments appear random and pointless to the medium so that she would receive no clue to the train of thought behind them. The script intelligences also suggest that their development of such an elaborate scheme would, in addition to demonstrating their continuing existence, also show that in their discarnate state they are not mere automata or sets of memories, but have retained the most significant capacities of the human mind.

They also spoke of the great difficulties involved in communications. They said that it is extremely difficult to use the brain of the medium to transmit messages because if the messages were very meaningful to her she would quite likely associate it with her own thought, resulting in irrelevant and misleading communications. Thus they had to conceal the messages in cryptic fragments. Just making contact with the living is painfully difficult, let alone generating a series of crosscorrespondences. The Myers personality, communicating through Mrs. Holland, repeatedly indicates this.

> The nearest simile I can find to express the difficulties of sending a message is that I appear to be standing behind a sheet of frosted glass—which blurs sight and deadens sound—dictating feebly—to a reluctant and somewhat obtuse secretary. A feeling of terrible impotence burdens me. . . .[25]

And again:

> Yet another attempt to run the blockade—to strive to get a message through—How can I make your hand docile enough—how can I convince them? . . . Oh, I am feeble with eagerness—How can I best be identified? . . . Edmund's [Gurney's] help is not here with me just now—I am trying alone amid unspeakable difficulties. . . .[26]

At about the time these messages were received in India, Mrs. Piper's Myers wrote that he was "trying with all the forces to prove that I am Myers." Whatever their source, these messages portraying such earnestness and effort are characteristic of Myers, who with dedicated intensity devoted most of his life to an attempt to demonstrate the reality of survival by the methods of science.

The chief investigators of the cross-correspondences were Gerald Balfour and J.C. Piddington. Balfour was an expert classical scholar and Piddington, too, had sufficient knowledge of the classics to understand the allusions made to them in the scripts. Both gave up a great deal of the latter part of their lives to a study of the scripts, with the script intelligences themselves taking an active interest in their undertakings. Also involved in a significant way were Mrs. Henry Sidgwick (sister of Gerald Balfour and wife of one of the purported communicators), Sir Oliver Lodge, Alice Johnson, Frank Podmore, and Richard Hodgson up until the time of his death in 1905. The difficult task which they had undertaken became a monumental one as the years went by. For the scripts continued to appear for thirty years and finally numbered more than three thousand. Over a dozen automatists were involved in their production. Some of the allusions to the classics were so abstruse that it took an expert classical scholar even to recognize them. In addition to this difficulty, the plan behind the scripts seemed to become more and more complicated as it became clear that the various quotations and allusions were not to be repeated in the sequel, but complemented instead. Thus the investigators had to spot the quotation or allusion on its first appearance and then watch for its complement later on.

APPRAISAL OF THE EVIDENCE FROM MEDIUMSHIP

We are now in a position to draw some conclusions. The fraud explanation is perhaps even more implausible in the case of the cross-correspondences than in the case of the other mediumship phenomena which we considered. To accept it we would have to suppose that the entire series was a most elaborate hoax perpetrated over a great length of time by a group of women of high personal character who stood nothing to gain—a hoax so expertly done that it was never detected by the alert and highly critical investigators who were in constant contact with the mediums. We would have to suppose that they accomplished this intricately coordinated cheating under incredibly difficult conditions, as they were scattered throughout the world and had to produce script after script containing allusions to matters unfamiliar to them while under the watchful eyes of the investigators. Of course, one could charge that the investigators too were involved in the hoax. But this is a desperate, "last-ditch" response which could be directed indiscriminately against any investigative effort whatsoever. It would be well to remember what Prof. Henry Sidgwick had to say about such a proposal:

> The highest degree of demonstrative force that we can obtain out of any single record of investigation is, of course, limited by the trustworthiness of the investigator. We have done all that we can when the critic has nothing left to allege except that the investigator is in the trick. But when he has nothing else left to allege he will allege that. . . . We must drive the objector into the position of being forced either to admit the phenomena as inexplicable, at least by him, or to accuse the investigators either of lying or cheating or of a blindness or forgetfulness incompatible with any intellectual condition except absolute idiocy.[27]

The total implausibility of the fraud hypothesis leaves us with only two: ESP and survival. Defenders of the ESP hypothesis have argued that one of the automatists, Mrs. Verrall, could have generated the cross-correspondences by telepathically influencing the minds of the other automatists. They point out that she was interested in psychic phenomena, she knew Myers and Sidgwick personally, and she was a very good classical scholar. However, if her subliminal mind was behind the cross-correspondences, an astonishing amount of telepathy would have to be supposed. We would have to suppose that for years her subliminal mind directed the subliminal minds of the other automatists as to their roles in a hoax perpetrated on their normal personalities as well as on her own. But even this supposition is not enough, for when she died in 1916, the cross-correspondences continued on in spite of the fact that there was no automatist left who combined her knowledge of the classics and the Myers group with the deep interest in psychical matters which could, allegedly, motivate a subliminal mind to work out such an elaborate plan.

It appears, then, that although the ESP hypothesis is very likely the best explanation for some mediumship phenomena, it is very implausible as an explanation of the cross-correspondences. Furthermore, as we have seen, it apparently fails as an explanation in the best cases of mediumship. An incredible amount of ESP on the part of the medium would be required, much more than is independently known to occur. The range of ESP required of the medium's trance personality would have to be *virtually unlimited*. The trance personality would have to have access to the minds of any and all persons who have knowledge of the various recondite items the communications contain, regardless of where those persons are located or whether they were thinking of those items at the time the communication took place. Furthermore, it must have marvelous powers of *selecting* out of that vast body of knowledge to which it has telepathic access, those items which are relevant in a given conversation at a particular time.

But even more difficult to explain on the ESP hypothesis is the dramatic form of the communications—the conversational give-and-take between communicator and sitter. As we have seen, in the best cases we find reproduced the dynamics of animated conversation between two friends who had shared various experiences. The communicator displays, with remarkable exactness, the memories, the temperament, the emotional sensitivity, and the manner of associating ideas characteristic of the deceased person it claims to be, as it engages in lively conversation with a long-time friend of that deceased person. To account for this, we would have to suppose that the telepathically acquired item must be instantly translated into the dramatic form it would have taken if uttered in that conversational context by the deceased person whom the communicator claims to be. We would have to suppose that when certain information is needed in the conversation, a telepathic rapport with the mind of the person who has it is instantly established, and the information is instantly acquired. But then the rapport must be instantly relinquished so that the information can be translated, instantly again, into a dramatic, highly authentic impersonation of the deceased person in question as he would have acted in conversational give-and-take.

Obviously, this would be an extremely tall order. Just the impersonation, let alone the wielding of an almost incredible amount of ESP, would be a monumental task. The psychologist Alan Gauld makes some interesting comments on this point:

> Some 10 or 12 years ago I spent a good deal of time studying the papers and diaries of F.W.H. Myers and Henry Sidgwick, thus learning a good many intimate details about their lives, characters, friends, families, and domestic arrangements. Yet I could no more deploy this accumulated knowledge to develop impersonations of them which would have passed muster before their close friends

than I could fly. The gap between accumulating such knowledge and deploying it in the construction of a realistic communicator is enormous.[28]

It is one thing to explain communications such as those claiming to come from Gordon Davis as due to ESP, and quite another to explain in the same way the lively conversational intercourse reported by Hyslop, Hodgson, Thomas, and Balfour. For the Gordon Davis communications consisted in the mere reproduction of voice characteristics and of two memories in the one brief conversation which Dr. Soal had with the Gordon Davis personality. And this is radically different from the conversational give-and-take reported in the best cases of mediumship.

It must be admitted, however, that at least one investigator familiar with mediumship phenomena opts for the ESP explanation. Prof. E.R. Dodds, in a paper entitled "Why I Do Not Believe in Survival,"[29] argues that the remarkable ability of the trance personality to select the items appropriate to the demands of the conversation and to translate them instantly into the form that the deceased would have given them in the give-and-take of conversation can be explained by supposing that the trance personality is *en rapport* with the telepathic agent to such a degree that it can select items from the agent's mind as quickly and as effortlessly as each of us can automatically select from our own minds. This explanation has some plausibility when the information communicated is such that it could conceivably have come from a single living mind. But it is much less plausible when used to explain communications such as those received by Hyslop, in which much of the information that he received was unknown to him at the time. For if we were to explain these on Dodds' view, we would have to suppose that the trance personality is *en rapport* with several different minds, and thus the task of selecting the appropriate items would be quite different from that which each of us is able to accomplish in the case of his own mind.

It is obvious that such an account must assume an enormous amount of ESP on the part of the medium. Such a degree of telepathic rapport implies that the trance personality virtually borrows the mind of the telepathic agent for the duration of the conversation, and, as in the case of the Hyslop communications, not merely one mind but several.

The conclusion to which these considerations point is now obvious. No one has ever come up with a hypothesis for explaining mediumship phenomena other than the three we have been considering. With the fraud hypothesis virtually eliminated and the ESP hypothesis strained to (or beyond) the breaking point, the only conclusion left is that some mediumship phenomena indicate contact with the dead, or surviving remnants of them. This was the general consensus of the investigators of the mediumship phenomena we have been examining. Hyslop, Hodgson, Mrs. Sidgwick, Lodge, and Balfour all eventually came to accept survival as the most plausible interpretation of these phenomena. As Balfour says of his sister, whose keen mind and cautious approach were worthy of the highest respect,

Some of you may have felt that the note of caution and reserve has possibly been over-emphasized in Mrs. Sidgwick's paper. If so, they may be glad to hear what I am about to say. Conclusive proof of survival is notoriously difficult to obtain. But the evidence may be such as to produce *belief*, even though it fall short of conclusive *proof*. I have Mrs. Sidgwick's assurance—an assurance which I am permitted to convey to the meeting—that, upon the evidence before her, she herself is a firm believer both in survival and in the reality of communication between the living and the dead.[30]

Even J.G. Piddington, who personally found the idea of surviving death distasteful, came to accept it. These investigators were people of high intelligence, they were originally skeptical of the reality and even the possibility of survival, and they were thoroughly familiar with the evidence for the existence of ESP and the way it could be invoked in an attempt to explain the mediumship phenomena they were studying. Yet they concluded that the balance of the evidence is on the side of survival, and that this survival consists not of mere memories or otherwise truncated forms of experience, but includes the most significant features of the human mind.

12

CLAIMED MEMORIES
OF PRIOR LIVES

IT MAY BE THAT IN THE CASE OF AT LEAST SOME DE-ceased persons, discarnate existence is an interlude or intermission which is followed by another life in this world. If we can conceive of this ever happening, we can approach the question of survival from another direction—in addition to inquiring as to whether someone who has died is still in existence we can also ask whether someone who exists on earth now has once been dead. In other words, we might look for evidence that some people have lived prior lives.

The doctrine that the individual "soul" lives several times on earth is often called reincarnation, but other terms such as "rebirth," "reembodiment," "transmigration," and "metempsychosis" have also been used to designate this view. It is a very widely held view. Though most of us commonly associate it with the Buddhists and Hindus of Southeast Asia, it is also held by many other people of the world. As Stevenson[1] and others have pointed out, it has been reported among such groups as the tribes of central Australia, and Ainu of northern Japan, many tribes in both East and West Africa, the Trobriand Islanders of the South Pacific, numerous natives of North America, especially those in Alaska, and the Druses and Alevis of western Asia.

As we might have expected, reincarnation is conceived in various forms. Some believers in reincarnation hold that reincarnation takes place immediately when death occurs (e.g., the people of Tibet) while others hold that it occurs several centuries later. In some views, everyone reincarnates, while according to others only some do. In some a person may be reborn as an animal, although in others this will not happen once the soul has reached the human level.

Although an enormous number of people believe in reincarnation of some form or other, it certainly may be that they are mistaken. Should we take seriously the doctrine of reincarnation? The most obvious objection to it is that the great majority of us do not remember having lived any prior lives. And yet if we had lived them, we might expect some memory. Now, it may be that only a few reincarnate, viz., only those who have some memory of a previous life. But, in any case, we must remember that lack of recall does not show that we have not lived prior lives. We do not remember the great majority of our experiences. But this fact provides no reason for thinking that they didn't happen. Positive memory can, of course, provide evidence about one's past. But absence of memory doesn't establish anything at all about it.

However, there is another objection based on the absence of memory which appears to constitute a greater difficulty for the reincarnation hypothesis. It is that if I have no memory of prior lives, what can it mean to say that the lives in question are *my* lives? What basis could there be for saying that *I* was reborn rather than that *another* person had come into existence? Two replies are in order. First, if I have had a prior life it would have been experienced by the being I find myself to be in my present experience. What I am talking about when I refer to an experience had by me, i.e., its belonging to the self that I now find myself to be, is indefinable in that no further account of it can be given. But then, no further account is needed, since each person knows from his own case what it is for him to have an experience in that unique and irreducible manner in which an experience is had by a self. Furthermore, he knows that there is a sharp, irreducible difference between *his* having an experience and *someone* having an experience of the same kind. He cannot deny that his being conscious yesterday is a different fact from the fact that consciousness was in existence yesterday. Thus it becomes clear that a series of experiences which were once had by me would be different from any series had by some other subject of experience, even though I cannot remember having had any of them and therefore would not now be in a position to tell that they were mine. For my not being able to tell this would not prevent them from having been experiences of mine.

The second reply is that memory of prior lives may be acquired at some time or other, perhaps between incarnations or at the end of the series of incarnations if it has an end. Such memory would obviously make meaningful, if not justify, the claim that a certain succession of lives is part of the history of one and the same person. Acquiring such memory could be experienced as analogous to one's experience of awakening from dream-punctuated sleep and finding oneself to be identical with the being he remembers himself to be in the various dreams. Successive dreams may be regarded as analogous to successive lives. In any given dream one usually has no memory of former dreams. Yet upon awakening one may find that he has memories of various dreams— memories which make it apparent that these dreams were experiences in the life of one and the same being, viz., his own self. So even though in any given dream one is not in a position to know that he has had previous dreams, this fact would certainly not be incompatible with his *having had* them or, indeed, with his coming to *know*, upon awakening, that he had them.

Perhaps the most serious difficulty in the reincarnation hypothesis is the difficulty in conceiving of what could transmigrate from life to life. It is obvious that knowledge, skills, and habits do not transmigrate; for an infant is not born possessing them. We are not born knowing how to play the piano, or how to solve mathematical problems, or with the knowledge that fire burns. No matter how many times an individual may have touched a flame or something hot in a prior life, he must learn all over again that fire burns. Of course, we *are* born with certain capacities to acquire knowledge and skills, and so it may be argued that these are what transmigrate. Furthermore, one might go on to argue that the basic set of capacities with which one is born is more important to the identity of the person than are the particular skills, memories, and information that he has acquired as the result of the interaction of these capacities with the particular environment in which his body happens to have lived.

However, there is still a difficulty to be met, even on the modest view that only capacities transmigrate. For this view seems to be in conflict with our knowledge of the hereditary transmission of characteristics. It seems that our basic capacities, or some of them at any rate, are *inherited* from our ancestors, rather than acquired or altered in prior lives and then carried over from those lives to the present one. Thus, at this point, it may seem that there is nothing that *could* transmigrate and that the reincarnation doctrine is, in the final analysis, incoherent.

Though this argument may seem to be very powerful, it does not conclusively show that no capacities could transmigrate. To begin with, our present knowledge of heredity does not justify the claim that all of a person's native capacities are inherited. Some, such as various physical abilities, are quite obviously a matter of biological heredity. But it is much less obvious that certain psychological capacities or predispositions such as to become interested in or have an affinity for something are inherited. Secondly, it is conceivable that some of the capacities that seem to be inherited are really not derived from one's ancestors. As the philosopher John McTaggart pointed out long ago, the characteristics in which we resemble our ancestors may be to some degree characteristics resulting from our prior lives. For, in his words, "it would be possible to hold that a man whose nature had certain characteristics when he was about to be reborn, would be reborn in a body descended from ancestors of a similar character. His character when reborn would, in this case, be decided, as far as the points in question went, by his character in his previous life, and not by the character of the ancestors of his new body."[2] The character of the ancestors of his new body would play a role, too; for it would be what would determine the fact that he was reborn in that body rather than in some other. Of course, McTaggart is not claiming that some of a person's characteristics are in fact carried over from a previous life, but only that the supposition that this happens is not incompatible with the facts of heredity.

It appears, then, that there is no real difficulty in conceiving of certain basic capacities transmigrating from life to life. But this fact would not justify the claim that we can conceive of the *self* transmigrating; for it is certainly not obvious that the self is reducible to a set of basic capacities. Unless we can conceive of the self transmigrating, the various doctrines of reincarnation cannot be considered intelligible views of the survival of the *self*. But this we can do. The conceptual framework for doing so has already been provided. All we need do now is draw out some of the important implications of the points made earlier about the nature of the self.

We have already argued that the self is conceptually distinct from its body, but now, for the purpose at hand, it is important to note that the self is also conceptually distinct from its mental or personal characteristics which apparently do not transmigrate. This distinction is not easy to express, but perhaps we can best get at it by raising the question as to what it is, in the final analysis, which distinguished one self from another. It is a question which must be posed from the perspective of the individual—what is it that accounts for *my* uniqueness. And the answer, when phrased in a negative way, seems to be that the source of my uniqueness is *not* to be found in my personal characteristics—in my interests, my desires, my knowledge and skills, my dispositions to think and feel in certain ways. This becomes clear when I reflect upon the fact that from my point of view (though not from the view of a third party) there is an extremely important difference between myself and some other person who might have existed instead of me—even if this person had physical and personal characteristics exactly similar to mine. If anyone is inclined to doubt this, let him consider whether he would be willing to have a truly identical twin exist not merely in his family but *instead* of him. He will very likely find this consideration to be extremely distasteful. The fact that the twin would have his personal characteristics would be no consolation worth mentioning. For his concern would be with the fact that *he* would no longer exist. Thus he will be led to the conclusion that he differs from another in a manner which is very important to him and which is unaffected even if this other self has personal characteristics identical to his.

Now, it is obvious that the source of my uniqueness cannot lie in my set of personal characteristics if another self could conceivably have the *same* set of characteristics. Nor, it would seem, does my uniqueness lie in *this* rather than *that* particular instantiation of a set of characteristics. Sometimes I find myself marveling that the unique self that I am is part of the world. I think about the fact that I might not have been in existence at all and wonder why I happen to be in existence. But when I do this I am not wondering why *this* instantiation of a set of characteristics is in the world rather than *that* exactly similar instance. Can I even sensibly talk about *two* mere instances of the same set? Thus I am led to the conclusion that I am a being which has the set and is conceptually distinct from what it has.

The implications for the doctrine of reincarnation are obvious. Even if it is the case that no personal characteristics transmigrate, we can nevertheless conceive of the self doing so. Of course, the fact that we can conceive of it doing so does not imply that this ever actually happens. But with this conception of what transmigrates we are at least in a position to make sense of the assertion that the individual self has lived several lives in this world. And since the assertion is meaningful, we are in a position to consider evidence that it is true.

EVIDENCE SUGGESTING REINCARNATION

Experiments with hypnosis and regression to presumed prior lives constitute some evidence for reincarnation. The subject is placed in a hypnotic trance and then instructed to go back before the time of his present birth to a previous life. Thought we should be properly cautious of statements made by a hypnotized person (since he is in a very suggestible state and desires to provide what he senses the hypnotist wants), there is good evidence that a hypnotist can bring forth memories of experiences which we would think have been irretrievably forgotten. One of the best cases of this sort was described by Morey Bernstein in a book entitled *The Search for Bridey Murphy*.[3] In 1952 and 1953 Bernstein was trying to regress a deeply hypnotized woman to an earlier life and then to obtain from her memories of that life which would be verifiable but which could not have been learned by her in any normal way. He chose Mrs. Tighe[4] as a subject because he had noticed that she readily attained a state of deep somnambulistic hypnosis, a state which he thought would increase his chances of success in his hypnotic regression experimentation. After placing Mrs. Tighe in the deep hypnotic state and regressing her to the time of her childhood, he then instructed her to go further back to a time prior to her present life and to report her experiences. She then began to describe various events of a life in which she was Bridey (Bridget) Kathleen Murphy, an Irish girl born in Cork in 1798. She made numerous claims about her life as Bridey Murphy, many of which were such that their verification or disproof seemed quite possible. And the search for Bridey Murphy was the attempt to find records or facts which would verify or falsify these claims.

Although many of the claims that Bridey made have not been verified, several have been and were such that it would seem she could not have acquired the information which they contain in any normal fashion. For example, she claimed that she lived in Belfast for much of her life and mentioned the names of two grocers—Farr's and John Carrigan—from whom she bought groceries. After considerable search by the Belfast library staff, these two grocers were found listed in a Belfast city directory which had been in preparation at the time of Bridey's death in 1864. Moreover, it was found that they were the *only* two individuals of those names engaged in the grocery business there at that time. Bridey also stated that during here lifetime a tobacco house and a large rope company were in operation in Belfast, and this too was found to be correct. Perhaps even more impressive are her statements about her life in Ireland that were originally attacked as being inconsistent with known facts about Ireland of that day, but which, after investigation, proved to be consistent with them. For an extensive and penetrating analysis of this case see Ducasse (1961).[5]

It seems that the best evidence for reincarnation consists in the various spontaneous cases of claimed memories of prior lives. Consider the following case:

> This I remember: a burning house, my home, my husband standing on the verandah roof surrounded by flames. Is he singing, drunk? or crazy? I run away from there, turn and look back to see it all.
>
> The house is on the edge of a wood and I stumble and fall by a stump. There are several centimeters of snow, a pretty little spruce tree grows by the stump. There I die: my clothing is nineteenth or the beginning of the twentieth in style. My age is around thirty-five. I don't remember any names, not even my own.
>
> My memory of something diffused and vague from the past has been there as long as I can remember, but this experience came when I was just over fifty years old. Then it came to me in a fully awake state; there it was, all at once, like when you pull the curtain up at the theater. I knew all the time it was myself I saw, and felt the pain and anguish the woman experienced, and the tranquility which came when she (I) sank down by the stump and everything was over.[6]

Though such experiences are intriguing, they usually consist of isolated pictures or scenes and consequently are very difficult or impossible to verify. By contrast, the recollections of young children which are suggestive of previous lives are often much more complete and thus provide the basis for a more fruitful study, particularly if the study is undertaken when the memories are fresh. In the typical case of this kind, the young child, usually between two and four years of age, begins to talk about the details of a previous life which he claims to have lived before the present one. He frequently begins to speak about this previous life as soon as he is able to speak, and, in some cases, his ability to speak is still so limited that he resorts to gestures to express himself and mispronounces words which are later understood better. The cases vary greatly in number of claims made about previous lives and in the richness of the memories involved. In some only three or four utterances are provided, while in others as many as sixty or seventy different statements referring to various details are made about the alleged prior life. And it may be that in all or almost all cases the child remembers more than he tells because of the negative manner in which others frequently respond when they hear such claims. It seems that even in Asia, parents and other relatives of the child tend to find such claims distasteful and either fail to encourage the child to mention such things or actively discourage such behavior. The fact that some children persist in making such claims, in spite of an apparently unsympathetic audience, indicates the strength of their conviction that they are remembering a prior life.

These memories apparently begin to fade when the child is about five or six years of age. At any rate he speaks about them less, and by the age of eight rarely makes any spontaneous remarks about a previous life. These memories are almost always accompanied by various kinds of behavior which are unusual for a member of the child's family, but quite in agreement with his claims about his previous life and often in harmony with what others say about the lifestyle and character of the person he claims to have been in the previous life. The child often displays adult behavior and acts toward other children as an adult would act. His memories are apparently so vivid that they cause him to regard himself as an adult instead of a child. He very frequently asks to be or even insists on being taken to the place where he claims he once lived and shows great concern for the people whom he claims he knew there. When taken to that place he seems to be familiar with it, perhaps re-marking about changes that have taken place since he lived there or correctly anticipating what will appear around the next corner. In many cases, he recognizes the surviving relatives of the person he claims to be and greets them with the appropriate emotions.

Ian Stevenson, whose pioneering work in this area is monumental, has collected data on and carefully studied a great number of such cases. Most of the children con-cerned are in India, Ceylon, Lebanon, Alaska or Turkey. But he has studied isolated cases in other countries as well, even in America and Europe. One of the many cases that Stevenson discusses in detail is that of Jagdish Chan-dra, who was born in 1923 in Bareilly, India.[7] Though this case is certainly not one of the more recent ones studied by Stevenson, it is one of the best authenticated, in that the statements made by Jagdish about his previous life were written down before any attempt was made to verify them and before the two families concerned had met.

Jagdish began to speak of a previous life at about the age of three and one half years. His father took an inter-est in the statements, recorded them, and then sent a letter containing them to a national newspaper requesting the readers to attempt to verify the boy's statements. Soon afterwards the father began to receive replies from resi-dents of Benares, the city in which Chandra claimed to have lived in a previous life. These people quickly iden-tified a man, Babu (or Babuji) Pandey, who corresponded closely to the description that Jagdish Chandra had given of the father he remembered. Pandey had a son, Jai Gopal, who had died some years ago and who was identified as the person whom Jagdish was claiming to be.

Jagdish made a rather large number of claims about his previous life. In addition to claiming that his name in that life was Jai Gopal and that his father's name was Babu Pandey, he said that they lived in Benares, that the Ganges river ran near the house, that the gate of the house was similar to the gate of Kuarpur in Bareilly, and that soldiers or guards stood outside the gate. He stated that the house had marble flooring and that there was an underground safe fixed high up and in the wall on the left-hand side of the underground room. He said that there were no daughters in the family but that he had had a brother, Jai Mangal, who was larger than he and who died of poisoning. He implied that he had been a Brahmin and that Babu, his father, was a panda (a supervisor of a bathing pier). He said that Babu's wife was called "Chachi," that she wore gold ornaments on her wrists and ears, and that she did the cooking even though Babu could have afforded a servant. He stated that Chachi made bread, observed purdah, had a long veil, and had a pockmarked face. He said that there were two persons called "Chachi" in the home and that the younger of these, with the pockmarked face, was his mother. He also claimed that a prostitute, Bhagwati, who was dark complexioned and had a strong voice, came to the house for singing and dancing.

Jagdish also made a rather large number of claims about Babu Pandey. He said that Babu had an ekka (a horse-drawn cart) and a pair of horses, that Babu was fond of wrestling and had his own akhara (i.e., small arena for wrestling), and that the latter received pilgrims (who had come to bathe in the Ganges river) in the big hall of the house. He claimed that Babu had malish (a type of massage) on his body, that he painted his face with clay or powder in the morning, that he wore gold rings on his fingers, that he used to sit in the courtyard in the evenings, that he drank bhang with his friends, that he liked rabri (a dessert made from milk and sugar) and took some arsenic along with it, and that he took opium every day.

All of these claims were verified as correct. Many were recorded in writing and verified before the two families met. Jagdish made a few claims which were not verified, but many of them are regarded by Stevenson as very probably true. When Jagdish was taken to Benares he recognized various temples, ghats (piers with steps to facilitate bathing in the Ganges river), bridges, and other buildings. He recognized the Benares Hindu University and said it was under construction in his time. He was especially familiar with the Babu Pandey home and the area surrounding it. One has to pass through a maze of lanes to reach the house. But the child pointed out the way through the labyrinth of lanes without any difficulty. He recognized Babu Pandey and many others. When taken to the Ganges where he had claimed he used to bathe, he seemed very familiar with the site. He recognized the Dash Ashwamadh Ghat from a distance, and gleefully took his bath twice with the assistance of an Indian whom he recognized at first sight. He was not in the least upset at the sight of the Ganges in August, which was swollen and flowing violently, making a terrific noise. As Jagdish's father was quoted as saying, "it seemed as if he and the river were old friends, though . . . he had never bathed in any river to our [i.e., his present parents'] knowledge."[8]

There seems to be no normal explanation of how Jagdish could have obtained such extensive and detailed knowledge of the life of Jai Gopal. Bareilly and Benares are large cities in northern India and are about 500 kilometers apart. Jagdish's mother had never been to Benares before the case developed, and, although Jagdish's father had been there, he had no detailed knowledge of the city. The mother claimed that the family had never even had any visitors from Benares. Furthermore, the two families concerned belonged to different castes, a fact which constituted a barrier to social relations in India during the 1920s. As we have noted, Jagdish claimed to be a Brahmin, as was Babu Pandey; whereas his present father was a member of the Kayastha caste. Finally, the family members assured Stevenson that up until the time that Jagdish's memories of a previous life had burst into full expression, he had spent nearly all of his time within the space enclosed by the rather high wall surrounding the family house in Bareilly. And when he did go beyond the enclosure, he would always be accompanied by a family member or servant. Thus it would have been almost impossible for a stranger or anybody else to have gained access to the child without his parent's knowledge of it.

It would seem, then, that there are only two possible ways of explaining cases of this kind: Either the child has lived a previous life as he contends or else he somehow manages to acquire his remarkable information by means of ESP. In the latter interpretation, he gets his information via mental telepathy or clairvoyance, or perhaps by a retrocognitive observation of the past life of a deceased person. However, the ESP explanation does not seem plausible in the light of the objections which can be leveled against it. If the child is receiving the information via ESP, then why does he identify himself with a certain deceased person? And why does the information that he allegedly acquires by means of ESP seem to be limited to what that deceased person would have known? Why does he have ostensible memories of the life of only *that* persons and not others?

Information yielded by means of ESP generally seems to occur in sporadic flashes. But, as Stevenson points out, in these spontaneous recall cases the child does not receive his information in the sporadic piecemeal manner characteristic of ESP. Rather, it is often detailed and connected. But, more importantly, he receives it in the form of *memories* of a past life. These experiences are as much memories as are his recollections of what has transpired in his present life. This is certainly surprising on the assumption that the information is acquired by means of ESP. Why should information acquired via ESP get construed as experiences of *remembering*? Furthermore, Stevenson points out that the ESP hypothesis does not account for the behavior of the child when visiting regions which he claims to have experienced in a previous life. When he comes upon some scene—say, a bridge, or building—which he recognizes and which would have been familiar to the previous personality, a new train of memories is generated, as though by association. And this is the manner in which memory actually functions. Stevenson remarks that he observed this phenomenon time and again. It is as though an adult were returning home laden with memories to the scene of his childhood and finding the various sights and sounds triggering a flood of additional memories to come forth.

RELATIONSHIP TO DISCARNATE SURVIVAL

In addition to providing evidence for survival as reincarnation, some of these cases support arguments for discarnate survival which were advanced earlier. Some cases of the reincarnation type involve an "announcing dream." An announcing dream is a dream experienced during a pregnancy, usually by the expectant mother, but sometimes by a relative or friend, in which a dream figure who purports to be the surviving personality of a deceased person claims that he is about to be reborn as a baby of the expectant mother. The case of Alexandrina Samona is a good example.[9]

Alexandrina Samona died at the age of five in Palermo, Sicily, on March 15, 1910. Three days later her mother dreamed that the child appeared to her and spoke as follows: "Mother, do not cry any more. I have not left you: I have only gone a little away. Look: I shall become little, like this"[10]—showing what appeared to the mother to be a likeness of a complete little embryo. Then the dream figure added: "You are therefore going to have to begin to suffer again on account of me."[11] After three days, this dream was repeated. A friend suggested to the mother that this dream should be interpreted as meaning that Alexandrina would reincarnate in a baby she would have. But the mother did not believe this because, among other things, she had had an operation which she believed would make it impossible for her to have another baby.

A few days later when Mr. and Mrs. Samona were bitterly grieving the death of Alexandrina they heard three unexplainable sharp knocks. They then decided to hold family séances, and at the very first one appeared a personality claiming to be the surviving spirit of Alexandrina. This personality purporting to be Alexandrina claimed that it was she who had appeared to her mother in the dreams and who had made the sharp knocks. She said that she would be reborn to her mother before Christmas and that she would come with a twin sister. In the séances that followed, she insisted repeatedly that friends and relatives be informed of this prediction.

On November 22, 1910, twin daughters were born to Mrs. Samona. One of them was named Alexandrina because she so closely resembled the child who had died. Not only did the two Alexandrinas have similar dispositions and interests, but there were some remarkable physical resemblances. Both had noticeable facial asymmetry, seborrhea of the right ear, and hyperaemia of the left eye. Both were left-handed, found cheese repulsive, were very much concerned with having clean hands, and enjoyed playing endlessly at folding and arranging whatever clothing or linens may be at hand. Both were neat, calm, and content to play alone. By contrast, the other twin was remarkably different physically, and turned out to have a disposition very different from that of the two Alexandrinas.

It appeared that Alexandrina II had some memories of the experiences of Alexandrina I. When the twins were told of a trip that they would take to Monreale, a place where they had never been, Alexandrina II asserted that she had been there before, accompanied by her mother and "a lady who had horns." Alexandrina II also described some of the things they had seen, including a large statue on the roof of the church there. The mother then recalled that a few months before the death of Alexandrina I they had gone to Monreale accompanied by a woman with disfiguring wens (horns) on her forehead and had seen the things described by Alexandrina II.

In addition to announcing dreams which suggest that discarnate survival obtains at least as an intermission or interlude between successive lives, there are many cases of the reincarnation type in which the subject claims to remember events which happened to him during the interlude between the time of his death in the previous life and his rebirth. He may claim to have observed the cremation or burial of his previous physical body and to have found himself in a different body between the time of his death and his rebirth. This suggests that he was having out-of-the-body experience like the person who, as a result of a serious illness or accident, seems to find himself out of his body, viewing it from a distance and observing what is happening in the vicinity of his inert body. We come to know about the experience of the latter when he recovers and describes it to us. But the former claim that they are in a position to describe what happens to those who do *not* recover! For they claim that they, too, were having an out-of-the-body experience while dying, but, unlike the OBE cases we have considered, they did *not* recover. Instead, they died, continued to have experiences, and then were reborn to find themselves with memories of these experiences carried over into their new lives.

SIGNIFICANCE OF SUCH MEMORIES

As we have noted, these accounts of memories of previous lives, if accurate, provide impressive evidence for thinking that some deceased persons have reincarnated. But it may be that we are not yet in a position to appreciate the full extent of their evidential force. Though the evidence may strike us as impressive, we may nevertheless wonder whether a person who claims on the basis of memory that he has lived a previous life may simply be mistaken in identifying himself with someone who has lived before. So let us examine the basis of such a concern.

As we have seen, memory provides us with an immediate knowledge of the past and in some fashion, without being infallible, provides its own guarantee. Of course, this does not guarantee that one cannot seem to remember something which did not happen. But, as we have seen, in the best cases indicative of reincarnation, a great proportion of the memories of the child were objectively verified. Furthermore, we saw that the hypothesis that the child acquired via ESP the information he seems to remember is not very plausible.

But the most important point to note is that memory establishes personal identity in the most complete manner, at least from the perspective of the person himself. When memory provides me with immediate knowledge of the past, I remember not only what happened but also my own unique awareness of myself at the time. I remember myself as the being I now find myself to be, and this establishes my identity in the most complete manner possible; for it includes the distinctive awareness that I have of myself at any time, now and in the past. It is the basis of my knowledge that I have remained one and the same being during the interval between the present and the event that I remember. Similarly, in the cases indicative of reincarnation, it is, apparently, the basis for the child's identifying himself with a deceased person. Thus whatever we think of claims of this sort, it is difficult to see how he could have a better basis for making them. That is to say, cases of this sort, if the accounts which we have of them are accurate, provide the best possible kind of evidence for thinking that the person having such memories is a reincarnation of a deceased person. Indeed, such accounts, if accurate, constitute an account of *what it means* to say that a deceased person has reincarnated in another body.

13

GOD AND CHRISTIANITY

IN PRESENTING A CASE FOR THINKING THAT WE WILL
survive death, I have said little or nothing about God and
how his existence would be relevant to the survival question. I have presented a case based upon naturalistic considerations alone—a case which does not depend upon
belief in the existence of a supernatural being, but rather
upon observations we can make of the natural realm. I
have presented arguments about survival and an afterlife
which are based upon observations of the nature of the
beings we find ourselves to be. And I have pointed to
various kinds of empirical evidence for thinking that some
persons have in fact survived death and have managed to
communicate that fact to the living. Though I have used
the term "paranormal" to refer to these strange occurrences indicative of survival, I would suggest that we
consider expanding our conception of natural law to include them. It may be that we not only came into being
in accordance with natural law but continue to exist beyond death in similar accordance, without this natural
process being willed or supervised by any higher conscious being.

It should be obvious, however, that if God exists and is at all like the Christian claims, his existence would be most congenial to the survival hypothesis. If God exists as a conscious being with moral concerns, if he cares for individual persons and is supremely concerned about their final destiny, then it would be reasonable to believe that he would prevent death from destroying us, if our survival did not come about in the natural order of events. A belief in survival founded upon the benevolence of God would not *depend* upon the findings of psychical research or the other considerations which I have advanced. But the latter are surely not in conflict with belief in God. They may be construed as indicative of the mode in which God causes or allows survival to occur.

It will be of value to consider in some detail the relationship between the Christian view of survival and the view which I have advanced. Christianity is surely the dominant religion in our culture and includes claims about survival which a great many people look to as the basis of their hope that death will not destroy them. Bertrand Russell once defined a Christian as one who believes in God, in personal immortality, and accepts Jesus as at least the wisest and best of men. Of course, most Christians accept much more than these three elements of doctrine, but Russell was trying to cite the main beliefs of all Christians of all persuasions. It is true that some theologians deny that a belief in personal survival of death is essential to Christianity. Shubert Ogden, for example, writes, "But what I refuse to accept as a Christian theologian, is that belief in our subjective existence after death is in some way a necessary article of Christian belief."[1] But this position is very difficult to maintain. A belief in personal survival is at the heart of Christianity, perhaps even more important for many Christians than a belief in God or Jesus Christ. Indeed, an impressive case can be made for holding that many Christians believe in God and Jesus Christ because such beliefs help guarantee the satisfaction of their more fundamental desire for immortality. As H. Congdon frankly states,

> The belief in God is simply not the most important belief they have. The real motive is nearly always the more personal one of survival. Suppose, for example, that it could be demonstrated that God does indeed exist, but we do *not* survive the grave. It is a possibility not often considered by Christians. It thrusts right at the heart of why one believes in God.[2]

Similarly, the significance of Jesus for many Christians consists in the way in which his resurrection helps to guarantee survival.

Central to the Christian view of survival is, of course, the event which has been called "the resurrection of Jesus." It can hardly be denied that something immensely impressive occurred shortly after the death of Christ which had the effect of restoring and enhancing his disciples' faith in him as their living Lord. If something powerfully moving had not occurred to lift the spirit of the disciples and cause them to publicly proclaim, in a most forceful and tenacious manner, that Jesus had risen from the grave, it seems very likely that the tiny Jesus movement would have perished with the death of its leader instead of developing into one of the major religions of the world. But precisely what that something was we cannot know with certainty, although we can lay out various possibilities and evaluate them.

Now, it may seem that the conception of non-physical survival which I have advanced is incompatible with the concept of a resurrection. However, this would be the case only if one construes resurrection as the resuscitation of the flesh and blood physical body. But it is certainly not necessary and probably quite unjustified to construe it in this way. There are other interpretations. Perhaps the resurrected "body" of Christ should be regarded as a non-material body, akin to what we have called an image body. Perhaps the resurrection should be understood as consisting in visions and auditions experienced by some of the disciples, experiences telepathically generated in their minds by the then discarnate Jesus Christ. More specifically, it is conceivable that the appearances of the risen Christ were truth-disclosing hallucinations in which telepathically received information is presented to consciousness in the form of visions or auditions. Though the visions seen and the voices heard would, on this view, have been utterly real experiences, they would not have been accessible to cameras or tape recorders.

Of course, there are other possible interpretations, but this is not the place to give an exhaustive account of them. What is important to note for the purpose at hand is (1) that the latter interpretation is the one suggested by the conception of survival presented in this study, and (2) that it should be acceptable to Christian faith because it implies that Jesus did survive death and subsequently interacted with his disciples.

But can a good case be made for accepting this interpretation? Isn't the view that the physical body was resurrected more plausible, more in harmony with the scriptures? The case for the resuscitation of the physical body is based on the gospel narratives. There the resurrected body of Christ is depicted as having risen from the tomb bearing the marks of the crucifixion. There we find the claim that Christ partook of food after the resurrection and invited Thomas to touch him. The view that the tomb was in fact empty is supported by the story that the authorities accused the disciples of having stolen the body and by the fact that it would have been extremely difficult for the disciples to publicly proclaim the resurrection in the region near the tomb (e.g., in Jerusalem, which was only about a mile from the tomb) if the body had still been there.

On the other hand, there is much that remains puzzling in this view that the appearances of the risen Christ were of the physical body that was buried. The first appearance occurred near the tomb to Mary Magdalen who fails to recognize him, mistaking him for the gardener (John 20:15). This is rather puzzling since she had known him well. He is similarly unrecognized by the disciples fishing in the sea of Tiberias (John 21:4). Nor do the disciples recognize Jesus on the Emmaus road until he breaks the bread (Luke 24:15-31). However, these failures in recognition would not be surprising if the appearances did not look or sound exactly like the physical body of Christ. Apparently, they did not behave like a physical body either. It is claimed that the disciples and others repeatedly saw what they took to be the body of Christ appearing indoors and then out of doors, irrespective of locked doors. Furthermore, the sudden vanishing of the appearance of Christ on the Emmaus road, followed by an appearance in Jerusalem, and then the ascension at Bethany does not sound like the behavior of a physical body.

However, such events would not be so surprising if the appearances were not of the physical body of Christ, but, as suggested earlier, hallucinations telepathically induced in the experiential field of the percipients by the then discarnate Jesus. For then there would be no reason to expect the resurrection body to appear or behave just like the physical one. And the various modes of perceptual experience can be accounted for, since there can be hallucinations of sound and touch, as well as sight.[3] This view that the appearances were of a non-physical body (understood as an image body, hallucinatory body, or apparition of the dead) is in harmony with Paul's claim that the dead will be raised in a spiritual body. "When the body is buried it is mortal; when raised, it will be immortal. . . . When buried, it is a physical body; when raised, it will be a spiritual body." (I. Cor. 15:42-44)

And it is in general agreement with Jesus' statement about the nature of people in the afterlife. He seems to be suggesting some kind of non-physical or spiritual body with his assertion that "when they shall rise from the dead, they neither marry, nor are given in marriage, but are as the angels which are in heaven." (Mark 12:25)

It may seem that the non-physical view is rendered less probable by the fact that the contemporaries of Jesus thought of the appearances as a resurrection and that perhaps all but the most sophisticated among them regarded it as a resurrection of the physical body. But this consideration really doesn't weigh against the non-physical view; for the resurrection concept was the prevailing Hebrew conception of life after death. Consequently, the appearances of the risen Christ would tend to get construed as a resurrection regardless of their actual nature.

Though the claims of an empty tomb support the physical body view, not much weight can be placed on them. There is an utter lack of facts concerning what happened to the physical body. It could have been stolen. Or it may be that the entire tomb account represents a legendary development. The gospels do not contain the earliest New Testament references to the resurrection. This is contained in one of St. Paul's letters to the Corinthians (I Corinthians 15:3-8) which was written about twenty years before the earliest gospel. In it Paul provides what is apparently an official Christian list of the resurrection appearances, but does not mention an empty tomb. Furthermore, his letter goes against the physical body view in another respect. He was apparently thinking of the appearances of Christ as visions or subjective experiences, for he regards his own subjective encounter with the risen Christ on the Damascus road as the last of these appearances. He construes it as a resurrection appearance even though he apparently does not observe an appearance of the body of the risen Christ. At any rate, he does not mention such an observation. As John Hick, in his scholarly analysis, sums up this matter,

> . . . at the earliest point at which we have access to the developing gospel tradition it did not include any empty tomb stories; and St. Paul's subjective experience was understood (at least by Paul himself) as an instance of a resurrection appearance. On this view, the entire cycle of stories about the burial, the tomb, the miraculous removal of the stone, the angels, and the appearance of Jesus himself in the garden—indeed possibly the whole Jerusalem tradition—represents a legendary development.[4]

Perhaps even the appearances of the risen Christ are part of a legendary development. As Hick goes on to say, "In the earliest experience and understanding of the disciples there was probably no distinction between Jesus having 'risen' and his being 'glorified,' 'exalted,' 'ascended to the right hand of the Father.' "[5] It is not my aim to try to settle this matter. I would simply argue that, whatever the factual basis of the appearances, the reports that we have of them seem more in agreement with the view that they were of a non-physical character, i.e., the conclusion that the facts and arguments which I presented earlier would lead us to draw, than with the view that the physical body was resurrected. Thus the view I presented in previous chapters is congenial to, if not supportive of, certain Christian beliefs about survival in that it provides a basis for understanding these reports which seems to make better sense of them than does the physical resurrection view, and which, at the same time, should be acceptable to Christians because it provides an understanding of the fundamental Christian belief that Jesus survived death and subsequently interacted with his disciples.

There are other points of congeniality also. What I have said about mind, consciousness, and self may help to illuminate Christian talk about soul and spirit. And my argument that the conception of disembodied or discarnate existence is intelligible is obviously congenial to the Christian claim that Christ was the Son of God incarnate, i.e., the Son of God temporarily assuming a physical body. For such a claim seems to imply that Christ was discarnate before the incarnation and thus assumes the intelligibility of claims about the discarnate existence of a conscious being.

My remarks about different spatial realms which bear no spatial relationships to one another can also be applied in a supportive way. It seems clear that the continued existence of the individual person requires some sort of perceptual experience. Some sort of environment must be perceived. Perhaps this is not a condition of intelligibility, but it seems clear that an afterlife would not be worth much if we could no longer see, hear, or perceive in any manner. At any rate, it seems obvious that, however vague a Christian's concept of an afterlife may be, he thinks of it as an existence in which he will continue to perceive in some fashion. But objects of perception are apprehended as outer, as being in space. Thus there must be some sort of spatial environment to contain the objects perceived, including the one which the perceiver regards as his own body. In this manner, the Christian would be led to conclude that heaven, or whatever he calls the afterlife world, must be a spatial realm.

But at this point an embarrassing difficulty seems to arise. If heaven is in space, then it would seem that it must have a location somewhere in our universe. But where could it be—somewhere out beyond the galaxies, someplace we could conceivably reach some day with a space craft? Such confusion exposes one to an attack of the sort advanced by Clarence Darrow when he writes,

If man has a soul that persists after death, that goes to a heaven of the blessed or to a hell of the damned, where are these places? It is not so easily imagined as it once was. How does the soul make its journey? What does immortal man find when he gets there, and how will he live after he reaches the end of endless space? We know that the atmosphere will be absent; that there will be no light, no heat—only the infinite reaches of darkness and frigidity.[6]

Any difficulty vanishes, however, as soon as we recognize that we can conceive of different spaces which bear no spatial relations to one another. Accordingly, we can conceive of heaven as a spatial realm which is not in the physical universe and bears no spatial relation to it, just as physical space and the space of our dreams bear no spatial relations to one another. And, in this view, it is obviously a mistake to try to conceive of ourselves traveling through physical space to reach the afterworld. Instead, we might think of reaching it in a manner analogous to our awakening from a dream. Thus we might regard it as only a change in consciousness away.

14

CONCLUDING REMARKS

WE HAVE TAKEN A CLOSE LOOK AT THE NATURE OF PER-
sons as we sought to answer the question as to whether
they could conceivably survive bodily death. On the basis
of a careful examination of what we consider essential to
our being persons, we found that survival of death is
conceivable and that we can form a clear, detailed conception of a Next World in which we could continue to
have experience in such a manner that personal identity
is unambiguously preserved. Then we examined various
kinds of phenomena which suggest that we do *in fact*
survive death and found that many constitute impressive
evidence for thinking that we survive.

However, it may be that the afterlife which we have
been describing is a temporary, though perhaps long-
enduring, state and not the eschaton or ultimate state
which we shall finally reach. That is, there may be development in the afterlife, perhaps culminating in what
the mystic talks about. Perhaps the claims of eastern and
western mysticism should be construed as evidence of the
existence of a state of being to which such development
is directed. Though the term "mystical experience" has

been used to refer to a great variety of experiences, what is of interest to us here are those which are described in terms of oneness and harmony with the universe. The latter experience is widespread, occurring in both Oriental and Western cultures, and in both religious and non-religious contexts. Its central feature seems to be the attentuation of the sense of distinction between subject and object of experience. The sense of the separateness of self and world diminishes and is replaced by an experience of total harmony, unity, and tranquility. In addition to the lessening or loss of the subject-object dualism characteristic of all ordinary experience, the mystic claims that the experience is beyond space and time. Furthermore, he claims that it is of the highest value; for it not only brings about "the peace that passeth all understanding," but it discloses the ultimate truth about the nature of reality. Unfortunately for us, the mystic cannot adequately describe his experience to others. He claims that it is ineffable. One must have the experience to fully understand what he is trying to say. But enough comes through to enable us to feel fairly certain that we would recognize the experience if we should come upon it.

It is not surprising that the mystical experience of unity and peace has been hailed as the supreme good and, consequently, the ultimate goal of human development. It is the final state of release (moksha) according to Hinduism, the Buddhist conception of man's final goal as nirvana, and the Christian mystic's ultimate goal of the unitive state in which human suffering in all its forms is finally transcended. As long as the sense of separateness exists, the world will appear to exist external to oneself as an object of desire and, consequently, as the source of suffering. Desires and regrets, hopes and fears, anxiety and suffering all arise as a result of experiencing the world from the perspective of a self separate from the world and concerned with its own well-being. Thus suffering is eliminated only when that perspective is given up.

It must be admitted that the mystic's view, to the extent that it can be expressed, has a certain appeal. But we must remind ourselves that a view must satisfy certain minimum conditions of intelligibility if it is to be acceptable, indeed, if it is to be a *view* at all. The mystic speaks of a disappearance of self and world into an undifferentiated unity. He ceases to experience himself as a self apprehending a world. As Tennyson describes his mystical experience, "All at once, as it were out of the intensity of the consciousness of individuality, individuality itself seemed to dissolve and fade away into boundless being. . . . "[1] There remains only the "Eternal One." But does it make sense to suppose that *persons* can participate in this? We are finite beings, and thus it would seem that any life beyond this one must still be some form of finite existence. Perhaps there is an afterlife in which takes place a human development whose splendors are unknown to us now. Perhaps it involves a profound and undeniable sense of the presence of God. But we could not become God or merge with Ultimate Reality without ceasing to be the kind of beings we find ourselves to be and, consequently, without giving up the notion that there may be a further destiny for *us*.

Since what we have been considering is the intelligibility of and the basis for belief in personal survival, it is clear that we must pay close attention to what we consider essential to our being persons. Since, as we have seen, consciousness is essential to the nature of a person, the survival of a person must involve some content of consciousness apprehended by a subject which is distinctly himself and no one else. And the presence of a content or object of consciousness opposed to and thus distinct from the subject implies that the latter cannot be unlimited. It is finite if only because it is limited by what it is not. At least this much seems to follow from the kind of beings we find ourselves to be. Thus if there is no place for this in the mystical experience, then it makes no sense to say that *we* survive in it—it is not *our* destiny.

However, it may be that the mystical state of the sort to which we have been referring need not be understood as involving the total annihilation of the self. Though the language that the mystic uses frequently suggests the extinction of both self and world, there are reasons for thinking that the most straightforward interpretation is a mistake. To begin with, the mystic usually ascribes the mystical experience to himself. He construes it as something that happened to *him*, not to the One. As Clarke succinctly puts it, " . . . they are not only described as *his*, but as his *experiences*, and this would make no sense unless we suppose them to be the experiences of someone, and this "someone" must surely be the person describing them"[2] Furthermore, it is obvious that when the mystic strives to attain the mystical state, he is seeking it for himself, not for someone or something else.

Perhaps even more significant is the fact that many mystics apparently view the mystical state as releasing the full creative powers of the individual, and as constituting the supreme enhancement of his individual being. They suggest that, rather than destroying the self, the real self is developed. In the *Dhammapada*, for example, it is suggested that the mystic, the tranquil enlightened one "who has attained the highest end,"[3] nevertheless remains a separate individual. Not only eastern but also western mystics can be readily found who speak this way. Ruysbroeck, the great Flemish mystic, tells us that in the mystical state he sometimes "felt" a distinction between himself and God, and sometimes a pantheistic unity, but that the former feeling represents the truth. The union of soul and God is like that of sunlight and air; though the sunlight interpenetrates and permeates the air, the two remain distinctly different things. And St. John of the Cross says that although on a supernatural level the soul is transformed or transfigured in God, its natural being remains as distinct from the Being of God as it ever was. He construes the union of soul and God as one of similarity of purpose rather than identity. Even Eckhart tells us that the mystical experience involves not only some sort of identification with God but also an affirmation of the life of the individual. Somehow they remain different even though they have become one. Though there is much that must remain obscure, if not downright paradoxical, about such utterances, it is clear that according to such mystics the experience of the unity of all things does not entail loss of the sense of one's identity.

It may be, then, that there is development of the self in an afterlife and that this development is of the sort suggested by mystics. Of course, such a possibility is contingent upon an affirmative answer to the central question as to whether there *is* an afterlife. What shall our verdict be? If persons were reducible to physical matter without remainder, the answer would be obvious. But since, as we have seen, this is not the case, the main obstacles in the way of belief in survival are the difficulties in conceiving of a non-physical afterlife and the apparent lack of any further contact with those who die. People die, their bodies decay, and that seems to be the end of them. The evidence of any conscious life has disappeared. But consciousness is a private phenomenon which cannot be observed from without as we observe bodies. Moreover, the self is to be understood in terms of it, rather than identified with the physical body. Even though we come to know of other people by observing their bodies, our concept of a person or self is not based upon those observations. It is based upon our subjective experience of our own selves.

As we have seen, introspection is the means to knowledge of the self. I do not learn what it means to be a self by observing others. For I have direct immediate knowledge of myself as a conscious being, and it is upon this that my concept of a person is based. I come to understand what it is to be a self, not via observations of the behavior of other people but on the far more adequate basis of my own conscious experience. It is based upon my observations of the conscious being I find myself to be. I observe that I can think of myself without thinking of my body, without thinking of how my body appears to myself or to others, or about the fact that it occupies space. And when I do think about it, it seems to be as subject apprehending an object. It may be that I could not introspect if I did not have a brain and body, but I certainly can introspect without thinking about them.

Considerations of this sort led us to the conclusion that the self is conceptually distinct from the physical body, however intimately related they may be. That is to say, the conscious self and the body are different entities, and thus it is at least logically possible for the former to exist without the latter. In this context we looked at a detailed conception of the self surviving in a non-physical world—a conception which enables us to know at least what we are asking when we ask about survival and which provides the basis for understanding reports of survival of death.

But, of course, the mere logical possibility of the self surviving the death of the body constitutes no evidence that this *actually* happens. What actually happens depends upon the nature of our world and, in particular, upon the nature of the relation between the conscious self and its body. In an effort to determine this we subjected to critical scrutiny the hypothesis that consciousness is produced by the brain and suggested some plausible alternatives to the production view. Then we engaged in a detailed study of various kinds of empirical evidence which strongly suggest that the conscious self does in fact survive death, and, in certain cases, manages to communicate that fact to the living. And these various considerations fit together to form an impressive case for the existence of an afterlife.

It may be said that we have not provided a *proof* that there is life after death. And if by a "proof" one means a logically compelling argument, then this certainly must be admitted. Though it seems that survival is clearly conceivable and consistent with what we definitely know about the nature of our world, the various kinds of evidence for thinking that we *actually do* survive death all admit of alternative interpretations. However implausible many of these alternative interpretations may seem to be, the fact that they have any plausibility is sufficient to render the survival interpretation less than compelling. But then, as we anticipated at the outset of this study, a proof is beyond our reach. Moreover, it is unnecessary. Good reasons for believing are sufficient and are, in fact, regarded as an adequate basis for belief everywhere except in the disciplines of logic and mathematics where one is dealing with necessary truth. They justify a belief without conferring a guarantee that it is true. We get along without a guarantee in the case of all our beliefs which are based to any extent on inference and evidence, though, of course, some beliefs are better justified than others.

It is obvious that a clearly intelligible and rationally based belief in survival has some important consequences. It provides a basis for regarding the world as a somewhat benevolent place, as more in harmony with our hopes and needs and aspirations than thinkers such as Bertrand Russell would have us believe. It takes some of the sting out of Russell's eloquent expression of his pessimistic view of our final destiny:

Brief and powerless is Man's life; on him and all his race the slow, sure doom falls pitiless and dark. Blind to good and evil, reckless of destruction, omnipotent matter rolls on its relentless way; for Man, condemned to-day to lose his dearest, tomorrow himself to pass through the gate of darkness, it remains only to cherish, ere yet the blow falls, the lofty thoughts that ennoble his little day; . . . [as] no fire, no heroism, no intensity of thought and feeling, can preserve an individual life beyond the grave. . . .[4]

Though we may have the highest respect for the courage and the honesty reflected in this somber assessment of the human condition, we now seem to have a basis for regarding it as overly pessimistic.

Certainly the thought of our impending destruction is the source of much fear, anxiety, and depression, even when not dealt with consciously, and it may profoundly affect our assessment of the value and significance of our lives. Undoubtedly, for a great many of us the primary source of the fear of death is the fear that we shall be reduced to nothingness—that we shall be obliterated from the universe. Death poses as the ultimate threat, the final negation of all our possibilities, the destruction of what is of most worth. It is the threat of our total extinction from the universe for all eternity. Many find it extremely difficult, if not impossible, to reconcile themselves to this possibility and would empathize with Unamuno when he exclaims, "If consciousness is, as some inhuman thinker has said, nothing more than a flash of light between two eternities of darkness, then there is nothing more execrable than existence."[5] For those who feel this way, a basis for thinking that death will not destroy us may be very uplifting. It may enrich our lives, opening up hopes and new perspectives. And if it turns out that we do continue on after death, then perhaps a cautious anticipation of this eventuality, along with a thoughtful consideration of what it might entail, will have placed us in a better position to understand what is happening to us and, consequently, to manage a little better on the other side. If, as a result, we shall be less fearful and less confused, we may then find ourselves with some advantage—like the one-eyed man in the kingdom of the blind.

NOTES

CHAPTER 3. THE NATURE OF THE SELF

1. R. Descartes, *Meditations* in *The Philosophical Works of Descartes*, tr. by E. Haldane & G. Ross (Cambridge, England: Cambridge University Press, 1969), Vol. 1, pp. 144-199.
2. D. Hume, *A Treatise of Human Nature*, L.A. Selby Biggs, ed. (London: Oxford University Press, 1968), Book 1, Pt. 4, Sec. 6, pp. 251-2.
3. H.D. Lewis, *The Self and Immortality* (New York: Seabury Press, 1973), p. 43.
4. H. Congdon, *The Pursuit of Death* (Nashville: Abingdon, 1977), p. 48.
5. C.D. Broad, *The Mind and Its Place in Nature* (New York: Harcourt, Brace, 1929), p. 623.

CHAPTER 4. THE ROLE OF THE BODY

1. We must distinguish between the physical space in which the material objects studied by the physicist reside, and the private psychological spaces in which mind-dependent but spatially extended things such as memory images and dream images occur. The existence of the former is inferred whereas the latter are directly apprehended.
2. The fact that consciousness is always of or about some-

thing is more technically referred to as the intentionality of consciousness. This feature of consciousness is, perhaps, the one most difficult for the materialist to deal with as he attempts to reduce mind to matter. It seems inconceivable that brain states should be *about* anything, just as it seems inconceivable that chairs, stones, chemical events in the pancreas, or any other material objects or events should be about anything.

Chapter 5. Is Consciousness Produced by the Brain?

1. W. James, *The Will to Believe and Human Immortality* (New York: Dover, 1956), p. 56.
2. *Ibid.*, p. 15.
3. A. Huxley, *The Doors of Perception* and *Heaven and Hell* (New York: Harper & Row, 1956).
4. *Ibid.*, p. 23.
5. *Ibid.*, p. 20.
6. *Ibid.*, p. 26.
7. R. Moody, *Life After Life* (New York: Bantam, 1975).
8. W. McDougall, *Body and Mind* (London: Methuen, 1911).
9. *Ibid.*, pp. 55, 69.
10. In further support of this statement, it is interesting to note the conclusions to which Wilder Penfield is led, as a result of his extensive exploration of the brain. Not only does his research lead him to a mind-brain dualism, but it suggests that "although the content of consciousness depends in large measure on neuronal activity, awareness itself does not." See *The Mystery of the Mind* (Princeton, N.J.: Princeton University Press, 1975), p. 55.

Chapter 6. A Conception of Surviving in Another World

1. H.H. Price, "Survival and the Idea of Another World," *Proceedings of the Society for Psychical Research* (London), **50** (1952).
2. R.H. Thouless and B.P. Wiesner, "The Psi Processes in Normal and 'Paranormal' Psychology," *Proceedings of the Society for Psychical Research* (London), **48** (1947), 177-196.
3. F.W.H. Myers, "On Telepathic Hypnotism, and its rela-

tions to other forms of Hypnotic Suggestion," *Proceedings of the Society for Psychical Research* (London), 4 (1886-7), 127-188.

4. Thouless and Wiesner, p. 195.
5. Terence Penelhum, *Survival and Disembodied Existence* (New York: Humanities Press, 1970), p. 103.
6. H.D. Lewis, *The Self and Immortality* (New York: Seabury Press, 1973), p. 81.
7. S. Shoemaker, "Persons and Their Pasts," *American Philosophical Quarterly,* Oct. 1970.
8. Penelhum, p. 56.
9. *Ibid.,* p. 56.
10. This way of stating the matter relies on a view for which I have already argued, viz., that the self is not merely a bundle of experiences but a being that has experience, and thus something in addition to the experience it has. And Penelhum would very likely not accept this view. But it is not difficult to show that even on the bundle view of the self we could have the concept in question and give expression to it in terms of the recollection of a disembodied subject. It seems that we can give expression to it by saying simply that two experiences, E_1 and E_2, belong to one and the same subject who remembers$_1$ some of his experiences provided that E_2 is a remembering$_1$ of E_1. It may be that no one can tell (i.e., verify) that E_2 really is a remembering$_1$ of E_1. But E_2 could nevertheless be such a remembering, and we could conceive of it as such.
11. D. Locke, *Memory* (New York: Anchor Books, 1971), p. 137.
12. Not only is the identity of a disembodied self not dependent upon bodily continuity itself but it seems that it couldn't be; for the criterion for something (say, y) is understood as it ordinarily is—as not merely a sign of y but that which *logically constitutes* y. For then it follows that those who claim that bodily continuity is the criterion for personal identity are claiming that what it *means* to say that two or more experiences occurring at different times belong to the same person is just that they are related to the same body. Thus, bearing a certain relation to my body is just what it is for an experience to be mine. But this cannot possibly be the case. For I can know that an experience is appropriately related to this body if I can identify the experience; but to identify it is to identify it as *mine*. I surely do not wonder whether an experience belongs to me, and then try to settle the matter by checking to see whether it sat-

isfies the criterion of being related to my body. To identify the experience in the first place is already to identify it as mine. Thus I must know without criteria that it is mine before I can know that it satisfies the bodily criterion (or any other criterion). It appears, then, that the bodily criterion leads to the incoherent position that I must be able to establish without criteria what can only be established by the application of criteria.

The bodily criterion also implies that we can make mistakes which seem impossible to make. If certain experiences are mine because they satisfy the criterion of being related to this body, then it must be possible for me to be mistaken in my judgment that an experience satisfies the criterion. Whether an experience does this would depend upon how things stand in the physical world, and thus would be a matter of fact about which I could be mistaken. It would follow, then, from this criterion that I could mistakenly ascribe a presently existing experience to someone else when in fact it belongs to me. But such a mistake is inconceivable. The notion of somehow being directly aware of experiences without knowing whether they are one's own is absurd.

Furthermore, the bodily criterion implies the obviously false conclusion that I cannot ascribe any experiences to myself. For if I am to do so, I must first establish that they satisfy the criterion of being related to this body. But even if it were possible, as it obviously is not, for me to establish that a group of experiences satisfies this criterion without first identifying them as mine, this achievement would utterly fail to lead me to the conclusion that the experiences in question are *mine*. For I could know that the criterion is appropriate for determining that the experiences are mine only if I am aware of them as mine prior to or independently of the application of the criterion. I would have to be aware of them as mine to recognize that the criterion is appropriately applied to them, and thus if I am to be able to ascribe them to myself, the satisfaction of the criterion cannot be that in virtue of which they are mine.

We see that these difficulties with the bodily criterion are what we might have expected when we recognize, as we did earlier, that the self cannot be known by description (or the application of criteria). For I must have an awareness of myself other than by way of description if I am to see that some suggested description applies to me. Thus it is understandable that if I am to see that a set of experiences satisfies some description or criterion supposedly appropriate for establishing that they belong to me, I must already be aware of them as mine. For a very clear and incisive treatment of these and other related points see *The Identity of the Self* by G. Madell (Edinburgh University Press, 1981).

13. One might say that memory provides the basis for *knowledge* of rather than the *reality* of personal identity, or that memory is a *consequence of* rather than a *criterion for* personal identity. If E_2, an experience of mine, is a remembering of E_1, then both experiences belong to me. But such a remembering is a possible consequence of both being mine rather than that which makes them mine. They are mine independently of my remembering them. Now, it is interesting to note in this context that Penelhum and others who argue that the notion of disembodied existence is rendered incoherent by the problem with personal identity seem to suppose that without actual remembering there could not only be no *knowledge* of personal identity but that there could *be* no such identity. But if memory is a consequence of rather than a criterion for personal identity, then their arguments, even if successful, would show only that a disembodied self could not have *knowledge* of his identity through time and thus would leave the *reality* of his identity intact.

CHAPTER 7. SCIENCE AND THE PARANORMAL

1. W. James, *The Will to Believe and Human Immortality* (New York: Dover, 1956).
2. John Beloff, "On Trying to Make Sense of the Paranormal," *Proceedings of the Society for Psychical Research* (London), **56** (1976), pp. 194-5.

CHAPTER 8. OUT-OF-THE-BODY EXPERIENCE

1. S. Muldoon and H. Carrington, *The Phenomena of Astral Projection* (London: Rider, 1951), pp. 194-6.
2. R. Monroe, *Journeys Out of the Body* (New York: Doubleday, 1971, 1977), pp. 48-50.
3. See, for example, H. Greenhouse, *The Astral Journey* (New York: Avon, 1974), p. 330.

4. E. Morrell, *The Twenty-fifth Man* (Montclair, N.J.: New Era Pub. Co., 1924).
5. Monroe, p. 75.
6. *Ibid.*, p. 76.
7. *Ibid.*, p. 85.
8. R. Moody, *Life After Life* (New York: Bantam, 1975), pp. 35-6.
9. *Ibid.*, pp. 50-1.
10. *Ibid.*, pp. 51-2.
11. E.J. Garrett, *Adventures in the Supernormal* (New York: Paperback Library, 1968), pp. 127-8.
12. Moody, p. 52.
13. *Ibid.*, p. 24.
14. Monroe, pp. 106-8.
15. *Ibid.*, p. 115.
16. O. Fox, *Astral Projection* (Secaucus, N.J.: Citadel, 1962), pp. 32-3.
17. F. van Eeden, "A Study of Dreams," *Proceedings of the Society for Psychical Research* (London), Vol. 26, p. 450.
18. *Ibid.*, pp. 450-1.
19. *Ibid.*, p. 459.
20. *The New Testament in Today's English* (New York: American Bible Soc., 1966), p. 397.
21. W.Y. Evans-Wentz, ed., *The Tibetan Book of the Dead* (Oxford University Press, 1960).
22. *Ibid.*, p. 2.
23. *Ibid.*, p. 158.
24. *Ibid.*, p. 182.
25. *Ibid.*, p. 156.
26. This quotation is from Swedenborg's book, *Heaven and Hell*. See W. van Dusen, *The Presence of Other Worlds* (New York: Harper & Row, 1974), p. 73.
27. As we shall see, this claim, along with others that Swedenborg makes, is in close agreement with a number of communications received through mediums and allegedly emanating from the surviving spirits of deceased persons.
28. C.J. Ducasse, *The Belief in a Life After Death* (Springfield, Ill.: Charles C. Thomas, 1961), p. 162.
29. Moody, pp. 84-5.
30. C.G. Jung, *Memories, Dreams, Reflections* (New York: Random House, 1963).
31. I owe this way of describing the matter to Michael Gross. See his article, "Some Varities of Out-of-Body Experi-

ence," *The Journal of the American Society for Psychical Research*, 70, (1976), pp. 181-2.

32. The cases of OBE, lucid dreams, and near-death experiences I have cited in this chapter constitute, of course, only a very small sample of the cases that have been recorded. And this remark applies to the cases cited in the next four chapters as well, those chapters concerning death-bed experiences, apparitions and hauntings, mental mediumship, and reincarnation.

CHAPTER 9. DEATH-BED EXPERIENCES

1. W. Barrett, *Death-Bed Visions* (London: Methuen, 1926), p. 11.
2. *Ibid.*, p. 14.
3. K. Osis, *Deathbed Observations by Physicians and Nurses* (New York: Parapsychology Foundation, 1961). Parapsychological Monograph No. 3.
4. This survey is reported in K. Osis and E. Haraldsson, *At the Hour of Death* (New York: Avon, 1977).
5. This survey is also reported in Osis and Haraldsson, *At the Hour of Death*.
6. *Ibid.*, p. 184.
7. *Ibid.*, pp. 87-8.
8. *Ibid.*, p. 130.
9. *Ibid.*, p. 168.
10. *Ibid.*, p. 190.
11. *Ibid.*, p. 129.
12. *Ibid.*, p. 131.

CHAPTER 10. APPARITIONS AND HAUNTINGS

1. A. Garrett, ed., *Does Man Survive Death?* (New York: Helix, 1957), pp. 9-11.
2. L.E. Rhine, *Hidden Channels of the Mind* (New York: William Sloan Associates, 1961), pp. 60-1.
3. F.W.H. Myers, *Human Personality and Its Survival of Bodily Death* (New York: Longmans, Greene, 1903, 1954), Vol. II, p. 28.
4. *Ibid.*, p. 28.
5. "The Chaffin Will Case," *Proceedings of the Society for Psychical Research* (London), 36 (1927), 517-24.
6. Myers, p. 390.

7. *Ibid.*, p. 391.
8. *Ibid.*, p. 396.
9. T. Moss, *The Probability of the Impossible* (New York: J. P. Tarcher, 1974), pp. 316-320.
10. *Ibid.*, p. 319.
11. *Ibid.*, pp. 322-3.

CHAPTER 11. MENTAL MEDIUMSHIP

1. J. Hyslop, "Observations of Certain Trance Phenomena," *Proceedings of the Society for Psychical Research* (London), **16** (1901), 1-649.
2. W. James, *William James on Psychical Research*, ed. by G. Murphy and R. Ballou (New York: Viking Press, 1960), pp. 104-5.
3. S.G. Soal, "A Report of Some Communications Received through Mrs. Blanche Cooper," *Proceedings of the Society for Psychical Research* (London), **35** (1936), 471-594.
4. R. Heywood, "Death and Psychical Research," *Man's Concern with Death* (New York: McGraw-Hill, 1968), p. 233.
5. R. Hodgson, "Observations of Certain Phenomena of Trance," *Proceedings of the Society for Psychical Research* (London), **13** (1897-8).
6. *Ibid.*, p. 328.
7. *Ibid.*, p. 328.
8. *Ibid.*, p. 406.
9. This is described by the Rev. Drayton Thomas in two S.P.R. *Proceedings* "The *Modus Operandi* of Trance Communications According to Descriptions Received through Mrs. Osborne Leonard" in Vol. 38, and "A New Hypothesis Concerning Trance Communications" in Vol. 48.
10. D. Thomas, "A New Hypothesis Concerning Trance Communications," *Proceedings of the Society for Psychical Research* (London), **48** (1949), 127.
11. *Ibid.*, p. 127.
12. C.D. Broad, *Lectures on Psychical Research* (London: Routledge & Kegan Paul, 1962), p. 280.
13. D. Thomas, "A New Hypothesis Concerning Trance Communications," p. 136.
14. *Ibid.*, p. 132.
15. *Ibid.*, p. 133.
16. *Ibid.*, p. 135.

17. *Ibid.*, p. 143.

18. D. Thomas, "The *Modus Operandi* of Trance Communication According to Descriptions Received through Mrs. Osborne Leonard," *Proceedings of the Society for Psychical Research* (London), **38** (1928), 52.

19. E.R. Dodds, *Proceedings of the Society for Psychical Research* (London), **45** (1938-9), 257-306.

20. R. Heywood, *Beyond the Reach of Sense* (New York: E.P. Dutton, 1961), p. 85.

21. F.W.H. Myers, *Human Personality and its Survival of Bodily Death* (New York: Longmans, Greene, 1903, 1954), Vol. II, p. 197.

22. Heywood, p. 102.

23. *Ibid.*, p. 103.

24. Broad, p. 313.

25. Heywood, p. 85.

26. *Ibid.*, p. 85.

27. H. Sidgwick, "President's Address," *Proceedings of the Society for Psychical Research* (London), **1** (1882-3), 12.

28. A. Gauld, "Discarnate Survival," *Handbook of Parapsychology*, B. Wolman, ed. (New York: Van Nostrand Reinhold, 1977), pp. 620-1.

29. E.R. Dodds, "Why I Do Not Believe in Survival," *Proceedings of the Society for Psychical Research* (London), **42** (1934), 147-72.

30. G. Balfour, *Proceedings of the Society for Psychical Research* (London), **41** (1932-3), 26.

CHAPTER 12. CLAIMED MEMORIES OF PRIOR LIVES

1. I. Stevenson, "Reincarnation: Field Studies and Theoretical Issues," *Handbook of Parapsychology*, B. Wolman, ed. (New York: Van Nostrand Reinhold, 1977), p. 632.

2. J. McTaggart, *Some Dogmas of Religion* (London: Edward Arnold, 1906), p. 125.

3. M. Bernstein, *The Search for Bridey Murphy* (New York: Doubleday, 1956).

4. Virginia Burns Tighe was born in Madison, Wisconsin, to Mr. and Mrs. George Burns. At the time she became acquainted with Mr. Bernstein she was married to Hugh Brian Tighe and living in Pueblo, Colorado.

5. C.J. Ducasse, *The Belief in a Life After Death* (Springfield, Ill.: Charles C. Thomas, 1961).

6. N.O. Jacobson, *Life Without Death?* (New York: Dell, 1974), pp. 178-9.
7. I. Stevenson, "The Case of Jagdish Chandra," *Cases of the Reincarnation Type* (Charlottesville: University Press of Virginia, 1975), Vol. I.
8. *Ibid.*, p. 153.
9. Ducasse, pp. 243-245.
10. *Ibid.*, p. 244.
11. *Ibid.*, p. 244.

CHAPTER 13. GOD AND CHRISTIANITY

1. S. Ogden, *The Reality of God and Other Essays* (London: S.C.M., 1967), p. 230.
2. H. Congdon, *The Pursuit of Death* (Nashville: Abingdon, 1977), p. 72.
3. There is, however, no clear-cut statement that the appearances of the risen Christ were ever touched. At the tomb he tells Mary Magdalen not to touch him, and Thomas apparently fails to avail himself of the opportunity to place his hand in the wound of Christ (John 20:27-8). Furthermore, the statement in Matthew 28 that Mary Magdalen and the other Mary "took hold of his feet" may mean only that they prostrated themselves at his feet in worship of him.
4. J.H. Hick, *Death and Eternal Life* (New York: Harper & Row, 1976), p. 175.
5. *Ibid.*, p. 177.
6. C. Darrow, "The Myth of the Soul," *The Forum*, 1928.

CHAPTER 14. CONCLUDING REMARKS

1. W. James, *Varieties of Religious Experience* (New York: New American Library, 1958), p. 385.
2. J.J. Clarke, "Mysticism and the Paradox of Survival," *Philosophers in Wonderland*, P. French, ed. (St. Paul: Llewellyn, 1975), p. 339.
3. The *Dhammapada*, tr. by I. Babbitt (New York: Oxford University Press, 1936), Chapter 26, p. 57.
4. B. Russell, "A Free Man's Worship," *Mysticism and Logic* (London: George Allen & Unwin, 1963), pp. 46-57.
5. Miguel De Unamuno, *Tragic Sense of Life* (New York: Dover, 1954), p. 13.

INDEX

ABOUT THE AUTHOR

DAVID H. LUND is chairman of the Philosophy department at Bemidji State University in Minnesota. He received his Ph.D. in Philosophy from the University of Minnesota.

Go Beyond the Limits of Mind and Body...